Emotions

PHILOSOPHY OF EDUCATION IN PRACTICE

SERIES EDITORS: MARIT HONERØD HOVEID, IAN MUNDAY, AND AMY SHUFFELTON

This series of short form books explores issues, topics and themes that are foundational to educational practices both within and beyond the boundaries of formal education. With books on topics such as collaboration, responsibility, touch and emotions, the series generates philosophical discussions of education that are accessible to the curious reader and draws out commonalities and differences in thinking about and doing education across cultures. By addressing educational thought and practice in a philosophical manner the series encourages us to look beyond pre-specified "learning outcomes" and asks us to slow down and explore the messiness and complexity of educational situations.

ADVISORY BOARD:

ALSO AVAILABLE IN THE SERIES:

Emotions
Philosophy of
Education in Practice

LIZ JACKSON

BLOOMSBURY ACADEMIC
LONDON • NEW YORK • OXFORD • NEW DELHI • SYDNEY

BLOOMSBURY ACADEMIC
Bloomsbury Publishing Plc
50 Bedford Square, London, WC1B 3DP, UK
1385 Broadway, New York, NY 10018, USA
29 Earlsfort Terrace, Dublin 2, Ireland

BLOOMSBURY, BLOOMSBURY ACADEMIC and
the Diana logo are trademarks of Bloomsbury Publishing Plc

First published in Great Britain 2024

Series design: Grace Ridge
Cover image © Tyas drawing / Getty Images

A catalogue record for this book is available from the British Library.

A catalog record for this book is available from the Library of Congress.

Library of Congress Control Number: 2024933291

ISBN: HB: 978-1-3503-4876-9
          PB: 978-1-3503-4875-2
          ePDF: 978-1-3503-4877-6
          eBook: 978-1-3503-4878-3

Series: Philosophy of Education in Practice

Typeset by Integra Software Services Pvt Ltd.
Printed and bound in Great Britain

To find out more about our authors and books visit www.bloomsbury.com
and sign up for our newsletters.

To Paul, Laat, and Geng.

CONTENTS

SERIES EDITORS' FOREWORD

Emotions is the third book in the Series Philosophy of Education in Practice. It is a common enough experience for both educators and those being educated, to find themselves bamboozled, bothered, or discombobulated by the kinds of thing that happen during educational encounters and settings. Trying to understand such experiences and acknowledge their meaning and import is something that can nag away at us. We hope that readers who are drawn toward exploring such concerns will find this book and the series to which it belongs, helpful in developing a deeper and more nuanced understanding of educational practice. Addressing educational thought and practice in a philosophical manner takes us beyond the sanctuary of pre-specified "learning outcomes" and asks us to slow down and explore the messiness and complexity of educational situations.

This series aims to explore the connections between thinking and doing in education through a variety of philosophical lenses. Authors will address diverse issues, topics, and themes, in multiple contexts, from a variety of perspectives. Throughout this series, we hope to elucidate the commonalities and differences in thinking and doing education across and between cultures. What holds the series together is not a particular point of view but instead a shared emphasis and approach. Each book will connect experiences (doing) and enduring questions in philosophy of education (thinking) to explore a major concept in education. Recent philosophical work has not shirked a concern with educational virtues and values, but its treatment of these matters is sometimes narrowly academic. We believe that educators, administrators, policy professionals, parents, and other citizens curious about education would benefit from a broadly accessible, yet rich, treatment that offers fresh perspectives on enduring dimensions of education. Whilst the series is designed to speak to practitioners, who are interested in reading theoretical work, the books in this series are not intended as "how to" guides—we would not presume to lecture to those working in the field, or attempt to find hard and fast solutions to educational problems. Rather, the authors in the series aim to philosophically inhabit practice and offer meditations on alternative ways of thinking/doing which arise from their research or teaching within the current neoliberal, globalized context.

In the third volume of the Series, Liz Jackson explores the theme of "emotions" in education. She argues that the dominant ways of thinking about educating the emotions tend to involve an overly narrow conception of what emotions are. Psychologists tend to focus on either academic emotions (how children feel about school) or on children's emotional wellbeing more generally. In both cases, emotions are seen to reside within individual persons. From this perspective there are "good" and "bad" emotions and education is about cultivating the good ones. Jackson argues that one dangerous aspect of treating emotions in this way is that children come to take sole responsibility for their emotional states and may come to blame themselves for possessing or choosing "negative" emotions. To address this concern, rooted as it is in thinking about emotions solely in terms of internal states possessed by individuals, Jackson argues that we should reorient our thinking toward seeing the emotional life as, to some degree, context-based. She argues that emotions are social in the sense that they are learnt during our ordinary social interactions, and that such learning must necessarily be shaped by sociocultural contexts. How we think about and experience emotions is therefore intimately married to norms endemic to particular environments and societies. From this perspective, emotions are not freely chosen, and individuals cannot take full responsibility for their emotional states.

Emotions has a rich international dimension. Jackson draws on her experiences of teaching in the United States, the United Kingdom, the United Arab Emirates, South Africa, and China to expose the problems with universal approaches to educating the emotions. Whilst acknowledging the dangers of national stereotyping in an age of globalization, she draws upon numerous practical examples to make a compelling case for seeing emotions as inextricably linked to social contexts. The international dimension of this volume is also enhanced by engagement with ideas drawn from Anglo-American philosophy, Continental philosophy, and Confucianism. Such ideas are brought into conversation with dominant approaches in psychology. Ultimately, Jackson encourages readers to think about what is at stake, practically speaking, in trying to create a culturally appropriate pedagogy of the emotions. Her exploration of difference, which considers issues of power and diversity within and across cultures, opens up a critical discussion of what we mean when we speak of "good" and "bad" emotions. This volume is a timely outward-looking contribution to an area of education so often characterized by the inward turn.

Ian Munday   Amy Shuffelton   Marit Honerød Hoveid

ACKNOWLEDGMENTS

I wish to thank the series editors, Amy Shuffelton, Marit Honerød Hoveid, and Ian Munday, for their encouragement while I was writing this book. This book was not easy for me to write, but Amy and Marit supported and helped me nonetheless during the writing process. The editors' detailed feedback and suggestions enabled me to improve the work significantly, despite my personal challenges and limitations. I also want to thank Mark Richardson at Bloomsbury for his collegiality, regular communication, friendliness, and overall moral support. In addition, Barbara Stengel inspired me throughout my writing process, with productive sharing, dialogue, and comradery. Finally, I am deeply grateful to Paul Trudgian and our cats Geng and Laat for teaching me so much about emotions and what matters in life, every day.

CHAPTER ONE

Introduction

In the last few decades, emotional wellbeing has become a hot topic in society and education. The relationship between emotions and education is usually thought about in one of two ways. First, some educators discuss "academic emotions." Academic emotions are interconnected feelings, moods, and attitudes students have about education and school. Well, academic emotions are the "good" ones. A student should feel alert and be open-minded, curious, flexible, resilient, and patient. These emotions and related dispositions can help them as they study, engage in school activities, think, and grow. There are also "bad" emotions from this view. A student can be too stressed out or too angry to get along with their teacher or other students and focus on what they need to do. Teachers and parents (as well as school leaders and school counsellors) are thus interested in the emotions of young people in relation to their education.

Second, there is rising interest in the role of emotional wellbeing in everyday life more generally. With the growing popularity of ideas of emotional intelligence (in the 1980s and 1990s) and resilience and grit (more recently), people are beginning to connect their emotions to their quality of life and success at school, the workplace, and at home. People promoting these views, such as positive psychologists, believe that having positive emotions leads to better outcomes. And they judge a life well lived as happy and emotionally fulfilling.

Education enters the picture here, because teachers can educate students to value positive emotions and be happy, "gritty," grateful, and resilient, rather than unhappy or frustrated.

These views of emotions are growing in popularity and making an impact in education around the world. However, they do not make up the whole picture when it comes to emotions and education. In this book, I explore these views, but I do so cautiously. One challenge to these views is that they both take for granted some basic features of emotions. As a result, both overlook other important ways in which emotions are part of education. In other words, these approaches get some parts of the story right, but they skip over others.

This short book gives a broader picture than most about emotions and education. In this introductory chapter, I will provide some glimpses of the chapters that follow, by exploring some other perspectives on emotions in education that go beyond what I have mentioned so far. This chapter thus aims to briefly illustrate what this book is about and why emotions in education matter. There are two major points I make here:

1   Emotions are social—not only individual.
2   Emotions are context-based—not simply chosen.

Exploring these points as they relate to education is my major task here. Another is to describe the rest of the chapters of this book.

Emotions Are Social—
Not Only Individual

The two common understandings about emotions in education that I described earlier—we can call them "academic emotions" and "positive psychology" views—are probably the most familiar perspectives on emotions in education to teachers, school leaders, and educational researchers. Both views are based primarily in the work of psychologists who have focused on the relationship between emotions and education or human development (Jackson 2021). These views have particularly shaped educational practices that aim to encourage and cultivate "good" emotions and discourage "bad" ones. Yet a common background assumption of these approaches is that emotions are individual experiences, as emotions reside "inside" persons.

Let us consider some examples. Picture a class of children, aged five and six. Some children are calmly listening to the teacher tell a story, sitting on the carpet, quiet, and passive. Others are falling asleep or drifting into their own thoughts, increasingly oblivious to the world around them. And some are being "naughty." Two children are playing a game by tapping on others when they do not expect it and laughing. Some around them, victims of their play, are annoyed that they are being distracted and becoming frustrated and angry at the "bad" behavior. Eventually, a few children become rougher in their play, anticipating more dramatic responses. Finally, there is an outburst—a slap, followed by a scream—that interrupts the teacher, making it impossible for him to continue story time. What would a teacher think and do in this situation?

In most cases, the teacher will identify and place responsibility (or blame) on the culprits who are (a) not learning or participating appropriately in class and (b) preventing or discouraging others around them from learning. The *source* of the students' issue is likely attributed in part to their negative or unhelpful emotions. They are restless, careless, and hyper, while others are, perhaps, too sensitive, or too easily distracted. So, the issue is seen as a problem of individuals and their actions, which are attributed at a basic level to their emotions. Maybe the whole class is punished after the outcry. But usually, only those individuals with the "wrong attitudes" are intervened upon (for example, through redirection or punishment).

Here, many teachers are not just concerned with stopping or preventing naughty behavior, but also with addressing the emotions "behind" or "underneath" it. They may therefore work systematically with a student who becomes well-known for her antics, to change her attitude or disposition over time to engage with others more effectively. The teacher may consult the child's parents about her behavior and where it "comes from"; she may be sent to the school counsellor or a special needs coordinator. The primary source of her problem, however, is assumed to be "inside" her. What is "inside" needs to be fixed.

Another example, this time from high school: a student is terribly anxious before giving a speech. He stands in front of the class speaking, but no one can catch all that he is saying, as his volume and pace are uneven. His face is rosier and sweatier than usual. His eyes dart around the room, hardly meeting his audience. Other students gradually start to jeer and giggle. What do you think a teacher would, or should, do in this situation? Some might ignore it and move on, feeling unsure how they can enhance the student's wellbeing, since he already seems terribly embarrassed and self-conscious. Others would try to help in some way.

A teacher could respond by discussing with the student after class how he can be less anxious in the future. A teacher could also give a lecture to the whole class which includes tips for managing emotions of anxiety and fear while speaking (such as focusing on one point in the room or on a friendly face and practicing extensively in advance). Still, the intervention here is at the individual level, focused on how students as individuals can fix their emotional experiences. The source of the problem and its solution are not sought out at a broader level—say, as an issue of the community (for example, students who as a group make a very poor audience), or in the more general context of the classroom (for instance, flickering light bulbs or strange electric buzzing noises).

A similar, but slightly different case: the whole class is anxious about their examinations. Individual students respond in diverse ways. Some are exhausted from lack of sleep. Others drank too much coffee or did not eat enough food (or healthy food) that day and seem erratic or hyperactive. Again, some teachers may respond to this situation, while others may not. Those who respond are likely to recommend emotional routines to students. They might advise students to try to relax before exams, not study until the last minute, spend time doing pleasurable activities, get more rest, and develop a positive outlook about the exam. However, they are less likely to provide significant classroom time for relaxation or for engaging in pleasurable activities.

These situations are common in classrooms around the world. They are cases that have attracted the attention of scholars and educators to the fields of educational psychology, school counselling, and socioemotional learning. That something problematic is happening with students' emotions is clear in these situations. And that something can be done about it also seems clear. Educators and scholars thus aim to improve these and other related situations based on their knowledge and previous experiences: for teachers, mostly their past work in the classroom, and for researchers, their studies and background training in their field.

While some people do not think of emotions as a subject in schools (in contrast to, say, English or math), the work of educators (and school counsellors and psychologists) to enhance students' emotional experiences so that they can learn and stay focused is essentially *education about emotions*. This education can be systematic, such as interventions put in place for particularly troublesome students, but it is often more informal and casual. For example, education about emotions can be conducted as an impromptu rant: "You all need to calm down!" Or, more gently: "Please pay attention, class." In many societies, this kind of emotional education is also being increasingly formalized as a curriculum for all students, rather than consisting only of off-hand comments.

I was a kid when emotional education was beginning to become concrete. One of its first iterations was "conflict resolution" (Boler 1999). The school counsellor came to my class once or twice per year to talk about the dangers and risks of "rogue" emotions, of anger, jealousy, and other related unpleasant and unhelpful feelings. Today, the only thing I can recall about this curriculum was a basic black-and-white drawing that our counsellor used, which was apparently of a melting ice cube on a plate. This image was intended to remind us to "keep cool"—to stay calm and composed under pressure. As girls in primary school (who were generally well behaved and mild mannered), my friends and I found the lessons laughably irrelevant to our lives. We secretly joked after each session that a person should always eat melting cheese whenever they feel upset. Though not particularly effective, this was a rudimentary education for socioemotional learning.

The field has advanced since then. Socioemotional learning, or learning for emotional wellbeing, is now identified as an important component of education by governments around the world, especially in early years. The lessons have no doubt improved (no more "melting cheese"). Textbooks around the world help students understand what emotions are, what they look like in themselves and others, and how to change their own emotional states. Consider the following lesson more recently developed for older students:

> If I identify that I am in the survival zone and that my adrenaline levels are high, this tells me that ... I need to do something to reduce my adrenaline (e.g. mindful breathing) or something to increase my serotonin (e.g. time with good friends, or seeing something funny), or both. By building up a repertoire of activities which I know to affect my emotions in predictable ways, I can start to become more skilful in the way that I experience emotion.
>
> (Harrison, Arthur, and Burn 2016: 135)

Again, such lessons teach that emotions are an *individual* experience: "my" adrenaline levels; "I" need to do something. We (as educators and scholars) tend to work mostly on the "inside" feelings, so that students can feel better.

Against this backdrop, this book emphasizes that emotions are not only individual, but also social. How are emotions social? Recall our first example: the young children getting in trouble for slapping and screaming at each other. Such incidents do not happen merely due to something "inside" the children. That is, the children were not at peace, until something (say, adrenaline) rose magically inside of them, spontaneously causing the outburst. Rather, the problem was always partly social in nature. One could argue that some of the children had tendencies or dispositions as individuals to act up (while others did not). But these dispositions or tendencies also developed within social situations (such as at home and in past childcare and school settings). And if the situation at hand was different—if it was recess, playtime, or physical education— their dispositions or tendencies would also change. And their "overactive" or "bad" emotions might be re-evaluated, as helpful and healthy even, rather than problematic.

Emotions are also social here (and they always are), because emotional expectations and expressions are *learned* by children in the first place. Some children *learned* prior to the episode to respond to other children and the situation by spurring and escalating conflict, by hitting back or screaming. Other children *learned* from prior experiences to avoid, ignore, or move away from the unfolding tensions. None of the children in this example may have had formal school lessons about how to emotionally handle such situations. But their actions, and the emotions involved in their actions, developed partly as a result of learning from previous, everyday social experience. In most cases, children's "naughty" behaviors do not simply stem from spontaneous rogue emotions bursting out from inside them.

Think about our anxious, older students. Someone looking at them from the view of academic emotions or positive psychology might say that they display "negative" emotions that do not help them in the situation. Some might say that the anxiety, nerves, stress, or fear which they "have" as individuals can cause them to perform worse. The student giving his speech freezes with fear, becoming indecipherable. The students with test anxiety are not able to focus due to their overly attentive, fight-or-flight states of mind (or exhaustion from stress accumulating over time). So, the typical answer is to correct the unhelpful emotional states at their root—with pre-test mental health strategies such as mindfulness, perhaps, like in the lesson plan shared previously.

On the other hand, a social psychologist would point out that while these emotional responses may initially seem unhelpful, they actually can serve useful purposes when appropriately channeled. The fight-or-flight response may make students look like deer in headlights, unable to focus on what matters. But if managed properly, this kind of response can lead them to focus *more* effectively: for example, to pay good attention to the time left for the speech or exam or others significant details about the context (i.e., information about the way their speech is being received or tricky aspects of exam questions). Some thus claim that it is natural, healthy, and useful to feel anxiety in these situations, and that something might be wrong with a student who doesn't feel such emotions in stressful situations. Again, the feelings or tendencies are responses to the situation—not just emotional phenomena randomly floating about inside individuals, striking at the worst time. And they reflect what people have *learned*, for better and for worse, to think and feel about situations—such as that the speech or test is important to their future, and that they should therefore make sure to do their very best work.

By neglecting the social side of emotions, educators and scholars who only recognize emotions as individual may overlook important aspects of student emotions and how education about emotions works more generally. At the same time, they risk imparting to others and teaching the lesson, informally and without saying it out loud, that students are as individuals entirely responsible for their emotions. Forget about Tommy tapping you on the shoulder and making strange faces at you all day long—*you* were the one that slapped or screamed. Forget the dubious expressions of bullies and other unfriendly classmates while you are giving your speech—*you* should "rise above it." Forget that this speech or exam matters to your grades, to your future possibilities to get into college, to your career goals—just "keep cool."

Thinking this way is attractive. Many people feel empowered when they believe they have full control over their emotions. This attitude can enable them to be proactive in relation to their emotional experiences and potentially be happier and achieve their goals more effectively. It also can seem more straightforward compared to other strategies, such as trying to change entire situations (like examination systems) to help students out. However, thinking of emotions only as individual phenomena also has downsides. In reality, few among us (if any) are totally in control of our emotions. And having absolute emotional self-control and using it to be calm and happy and achievement-oriented in every situation is also not entirely healthy. In addition, focusing primarily on the importance and benefits of emotional self-regulation and self-control can unintentionally teach people to sometimes *feel bad* about their emotions. It can teach people that they are to blame if they experience negative emotions in response to uncontrollable things that happen to them in life, although we all inevitably face challenges and problems. This relates to the second limitation to common ways of thinking about emotions in education.

Emotions Are Context-Based— Not Simply Chosen

I have already mentioned here that people's feelings are related to social situations and the actions of others. And that emotions are *learned*. They are learned in a way that goes beyond school subjects or lesson plans, at a deep level, because emotions are profoundly social in nature. In relation, emotions are *context-based*. That is, the cultural and social environment makes a difference for how emotions are understood and learned in and through relationships with others. As a result, emotions are not thought about or experienced the same way across all people and cultures. Therefore, people cannot simply pick their emotions as if they come from a menu, despite the assumptions of some people coming from academic emotions and positive psychology views.

There are two major ways that context matters here. *First*, context matters in relation to emotions and how they are basically understood at a broad, cultural level. Consider the role of happiness in education. Happiness is highly valued in many societies and schools. Noddings' book *Happiness and Education* has led many readers (particularly in North America but also elsewhere around the world) to believe that schools should focus more on happiness (2003). However, the educational goal of happiness, and the view of happiness as an individual emotional experience, is not as commonly recognized in East Asian societies. In relation, if you ask people in China and the United States what happiness means to them, you will get different responses. In Western countries, there tends to be a focus on personal feelings and judgments about living a good, pleasant, meaningful, or fulfilling life, at the individual level. In China, an assessment is more likely to be given that is social in nature, related to being in a good family, surrounded by healthy, flourishing people, and contributing to the community (i.e., Ho, Duan and Tang 2014).

Some people may have been taught such meanings of happiness explicitly in school. But most people learn to see happiness in these different ways through informal socialization and development, through interpersonal relationships starting in early childhood. In China, a child may learn through interactions with her family and teachers that it is cheeky or even rude to "show off" and be pleased with herself as an individual, especially when others are experiencing problems. She is thus informally taught not to be too personally proud or arrogant about her achievements, because they are understood to partly be the result of the efforts of her parents and teachers, which she should pay back by diligently and gratefully contributing to her family, school, and society (Harrison et al. 2023). So, over time she learns to feel and express happiness only when the whole class does well, or after her parents or teachers indicate they are pleased with her achievements. Meanwhile, a child in the United States is more likely to be encouraged by parents and teachers to take *personal* pride in her achievements: to smile, perhaps boast, feel good, and share about her success with others in a carefree way, which becomes even better in a competitive environment, where she as an individual performed better than others.

My point here is not that the definition or understanding of happiness between China and the United States is totally, fundamentally incommensurable. Or that the feelings or definitions of happiness are mutually exclusive or clashing in an essential way. Such arguments are not necessary to make, and (in a world with porous borders and global interconnection) I doubt they are true, regardless. Rather, my point here is that people's understandings and experiences related to emotions are not selected as freely as some scholars (and some lessons) seem to suggest. As emotions are learned, they are learned in culturally unique ways.

This cultural context has important implications for educating about emotions in informal and formal ways in schools that include students from varied backgrounds. For instance, a child whose family has recently moved from China to the United States might not benefit as much as other children do from her teacher encouraging or expecting her to experience and express exuberant personal pride in her test scores. Such encouragement could be well-intentioned and help the student to feel good about herself and relate positively to her teacher and her classmates. However, the student coming from China nonetheless has cross-cultural complications to grapple with. If she complies whole-heartedly with her teachers' expectations, she could get into (minor) trouble with her family elders when she gets home and neglects to thank them in a serious and respectful manner (as is commonly expected in Chinese societies) for their contributions to her success. Facing this mismatch in expectations, the teacher's encouragement of personal pride and self-satisfaction could also leave the student confused, wondering why her teacher would want her to express herself in an arrogant way that could displease her family.

Across societies, such mismatches can be addressed in terms of culturally appropriate pedagogy, among educators concerned with new immigrant and ethnic minority experiences of not fitting in within mainstream norms which often go unnoticed by members of majority groups. However, these approaches often tend to focus on surface-level expressions of emotions, like whether students are comfortable making sustained eye contact with teachers. Meanwhile, the deeper aspects of emotional diversity often go unnoticed. This is because many scholars tend to focus, either out of convenience or in attempts to conduct efficient research, only on their own culture in examining emotions, considering cultural differences as anomalies from norms. At the same time, few people realize how they themselves learned about emotions within a thick cultural context. They assume that emotions are basically similar the world over, lacking experiences that teach them otherwise.

I lived in many different countries around the world—the United States, the United Kingdom, South Africa, the United Arab Emirates, and China—before I started reflecting deeply on global diversity in emotional experiences and expressions. I had been teaching at the University of Hong Kong for several years before I realized how profoundly my own cultural assumptions made a difference (Jackson 2023). One day in class, my students looked more tense and anxious than usual. It seemed that confusion about my lesson was increasing their stress. Then I did something that I had often done before in classrooms, in other parts of the world. I asked my students to take a break, thinking it would help them relax to stand up and walk around or buy a snack or drink nearby. However, in this case, not a single student rose from their seat.

Sensing that my intention was not being grasped and feeling worse about my part in the situation, I then "gently" commanded them to all stand up, to stop looking at their laptops or readings, and to stretch out their bodies with some simple yoga poses—something that seemed to help many of my students and improve the classroom experience in the past, in such contexts as the United States and in South Africa. My students then looked more miserable than ever before. They seemed embarrassed, ashamed, and uncomfortable. I realized then how my assumptions about how one should *feel* when learning, and how they should relate to their educator, were the opposite of those of my Hong Kong students. Instead of enhancing the situation, I was making it worse. By responding proactively and intervening, I was expressing that there was a problem. In this case, given my students' past experiences with education throughout their lives, they felt that the point of the exercise was that *they* were doing something wrong—yet in my mind, I was clearly the source of the problem.

Even after living outside the United States for fifteen years, my understanding of the right emotions to feel and express in education remains ingrained from my own childhood experiences and largely beyond my awareness. I learned in that moment that none of us can choose our emotions freely or simply code-switch once we technically understand more, because our emotions are related to our deeply held beliefs and values, which underlie our approaches to education, learning and teaching, and the development of all sorts of relationships. In this context, I realized for the first time how many "ordinary" classrooms contain significant invisible emotional diversity and complexity that gets overlooked every day by teachers (and students) who take for granted their own cultural norms, as well as the ease and simplicity of cross-cultural adaptation.

These examples also hint at different ways of understanding social roles in society. In the last examples, it is not only the case that the nature of happiness (and studiousness) is thought about and taught about differently across cultural groups. It is also that social relations within communities, and the role of emotions in social relations (i.e., of child and elder or student and teacher), are thought about and taught about differently. Thus, the *second* way that context matters in developing and educating emotions is in relation to social roles and power relationships.

One of my favorite examples here relates to McDonald's and "service with a smile" in Hong Kong (Watson 2006). Large, open-mouthed smiles generally equal welcoming, caring, and all going well in the United States. However, in Hong Kong mouthy smiles are more often associated with carelessness, goofiness, and other emotions and dispositions basically at odds with traditional virtues of duty, sobriety (or seriousness), and respect. Greeting customers with an open-mouth smile at McDonald's in Hong Kong was therefore not experienced by local customers as welcoming or serving, but as something closer to their opposite—aloofness, nonchalance, or uncaring. Good service matters in both places—as does being caring and welcoming, through emotional expressions and related behavior. But the details in real-life situations are different. As McDonald's had to rethink "service with a smile" abroad, so should scholars and teachers reflect upon their assumptions about emotions in education as contextually based.

The cultural context of emotions is one marked by power relations (Boler 1999). Here, we have touched on the relations of teachers with students, children with parents, and customers with McDonald's employees. These are not entirely equal relations. In some sense they are hierarchical ones, where one person has more authority or power than another. But there are other, even more complicated power relations to consider. Take our first-generation Chinese American schoolgirl. I will argue in this text that it matters that she is a girl (i.e., that she is seen and identified by others and herself as a girl), because boys across cultures are encouraged to be more boisterous, proud, and independent-minded than girls. Again, people typically learn these differences not by being taught about them through lectures or textbooks (although they might have been in the past), but through informal, everyday life experiences starting in childhood, where their pride or humility is encouraged or discouraged systematically, usually in hidden ways, over years.

People learn what emotions to have and how to express them—at home and in school. And each person learns slightly different things, because each has a slightly different experience. And part of each person's experience is that they are treated differently by others partly based of their unasked-for personal characteristics. These include gender as well as other identity factors: race and ethnicity, social class, language, ability, and more. In other words, people expect different emotions from others based on gender, race, and class. For instance, while an angry white man may be commended in news media for being passionate and committed to his cause (think of any politician in a Western society here), a Black man expressing himself in the same way is more likely to be described as hostile, irrational, or violent (Gay 2016). People learn from these examples, as they learn over the course of their lives which emotions are expected and accepted from themselves and others. Again, this inequality in emotional expectations means that none of us are entirely free to choose our emotions, as if they come from a menu. Or, maybe we can pick our emotions from a menu. But we all have different menus. And you cannot simply exchange your menu for a better one.

That emotions are social within a context marked by diverse cultures, identities, and power relations means that the way educators teach about, and more subtly teach, manage, and "work on" young people's emotions is a moral and political issue. Is it right to encourage boys to be prouder than girls? To encourage white boys to be angrier than Black boys? Arguably not. To "teach" emotions in these ways is to limit or fix the menu (or spectrum) of opportunities for youth socioemotional development based on gender or racial bias. And to perpetuate a status quo (and teach to students) that not everyone is equally allowed to express their feelings. Thus, educators and scholars concerned with educating emotions formally and informally should consider more deeply how emotions are educated inside and outside of classrooms. Educators interested in socioemotional wellbeing, academic emotions, and related areas want to make a positive difference in students' lives. Understanding more critically what emotions are and how they operate and are learned can no doubt help with this work, for the wellbeing of all people at personal and social levels. These points inspire this text.

What Lies Ahead

This chapter aimed to give a taste of what this book is about. The chapters that follow go into more detail about various issues involved in teaching about emotions. The next (second) chapter more fully responds to the question of what emotions are and why and how they matter. Contrary to what some might imagine, what emotions are and why they matter is contested across disciplines and cultures. Understanding some of the complexity about defining emotions helps us recognize and begin to grapple with the importance of different ways of seeing and shaping emotions in education. Thus, in this chapter I examine psychological and Western and Eastern philosophical views of emotions. Then I introduce another way of thinking about emotions which I discuss as "the politics of emotions." This latter view more critically investigates the "inward turn" in thinking about education for wellbeing as an individual responsibility.

The third and fourth chapters look at individual emotions in education in a more systematic way, considering how so-called positive and negative emotions are understood and taught about in schools. The third chapter focuses on happiness, compassion, empathy, caring, and gratitude. It aims to provide a more balanced and critical view of these emotions and their place in education, by observing some of the challenges and pitfalls, as well as the potential, in teaching for and about them. The fourth chapter looks at "negative" emotions, including anger, sadness, fear, and anxiety, again more holistically considering their value as well as some of the risks and challenges in teaching about them. The conclusion of this book, the fifth chapter, revisits emotional wellbeing in education and the politics of the inward turn overall, exploring recent related hype around resilience, mindfulness, and grit. It summarizes the major points of this text and provides a final account of the importance of educating emotions for wellbeing and social and civic engagement.

CHAPTER TWO

What Are Emotions?

What are emotions? Most people take the answer to this question for granted. You might have learned a definition of emotions in school, and—depending upon where and when you grew up—you may have learned to identify and list out some emotions and distinguish what emotions are from what they are not: for example, "scared" is an emotion, but "funny" is not. But apart from that, we learn much more about emotions, including what they are, what they mean, and why they matter, through the course of normal life. Thus, what we know (or think we know) about emotions is, for most of us, a largely unexamined bundle of assumptions and beliefs that help us get on with life, without constantly questioning every aspect of it.

I never thought much about emotions (mine or those of others) when I was growing up. As mentioned in the Introduction, I was taught the importance of "keeping cool" in conflict resolution lessons in elementary school, but these lessons seemed totally irrelevant to my life, as I did not have a problem with keeping cool. I only started thinking about emotions as I developed as a philosopher interested in morality and ethics and as I started learning more about myself and my emotions while receiving counselling during my divorce. Before then, I simply thought that my emotions were either helpful or harmful: helpful when they assist me to complete goals, such as when I am driven, focused, and dedicated, and harmful when they distract me from the things I want to do, such as when they hinder my ability to think rationally, persist with work tasks, or focus on my goals (Jackson 2023).

Without knowing it, I was influenced by a highly particular understanding of emotions, as individually based and freely chosen. Working with a counsellor initiated a journey for me, however, to realize that my emotions and how they work are influenced by much more than that: by family and childhood experiences, personal identity, and interpersonal relationships. In this context, I cannot (much as I would like to) just choose the best emotions from a menu ("I'll take the all-you-can-feel joy and calm—no ice") and refuse the emotions I want to discard ("Leave the anxiety and frustration on the side"). This was a big learning curve for me. I suddenly realized I had many assumptions about emotions that I had never really thought about, some of which were not helpful to me.

One's understanding of emotions is at the heart of any idea they have about the role emotions play in education and the nature of education for emotional development and wellbeing. However, what emotions are and how they work are not settled questions. Actually, there are diverse, clashing views. In some, such as in psychology, emotions are considered separately from ethical and moral matters, while in others, such as in virtue ethics, emotions and ethics are closely intertwined. These differences have implications for how emotions are thought about and taught about in education, in formal and informal lessons by teachers and other caregivers.

In this chapter, I take a deep dive into what emotions are across academic fields and global traditions, including psychology and Western and Eastern philosophical views. Then I discuss another perspective which I call the "politics of emotions" (Ahmed 2004a; Jackson 2021). This chapter thus compares views that inform people's assumptions about emotions that they carry into everyday life, including education. And it shows how the ground underneath educators working to help students learn about their emotions is shaky, where many points are still hotly debated.

Psychological Views

Psychological views about emotions are the most prominent in education. To understand psychological views of emotions, consider psychology more generally. Psychologists focus on the mind and behavior in relation to the "inner" "functioning" of people as individuals. Historically, considering human dysfunction inspired many people in psychology in the first place. Dysfunction is what interested Freud when he founded psychoanalysis, the practice of treating problems of the "psyche," or the conscious and unconscious aspects and operations of the mind. In his work, Freud identified and studied problematic emotional conditions of hysteria, psychopathy, repression, neurosis, anxiety, paranoia, and nervousness. Although his work and theories are controversial, his argument that humans have biological or physical "drives" which they rationalize to function in society fits to some extent with mainstream psychological views of emotions today.

For contemporary psychologists, emotions are subjective feeling responses to external or internal stimuli, accompanied by evaluative cognitive judgments and interpretations. Internal stimuli include drives or impulses related to neurophysiological changes over which people typically have little to no control: for example, heart rate, hormonal, sensory, or body temperature changes (Shuman and Scherer 2014). A person experiences these changes while facing situations in their environment. A student giving a speech or preparing for an exam may experience hyperawareness of his surroundings, a quickening heart rate, and pupil dilation. The "making sense" of this cognitively—the student asking himself what he is feeling and why—results in him identifying the emotional state: anxiety or fear. Feeling or "affect" is positioned somewhere between drives and interpretations.

Psychologists regard it as functional to experience appropriate emotions in different situations. Ideally, the (slightly) hyperactive experience of exam anxiety can increase alertness and help a person avoid mistakes. Meanwhile, feeling carefree or depressed during a test could signal emotional dysfunction, because these experiences are not regarded as typical or sensible and can get in the way of success.

I was taught to "cool off" in school-based conflict resolution, which aimed to reduce student interpersonal problems and keep us focused on schoolwork. Earlier in the United States, in the late nineteenth and early twentieth centuries, "mental hygiene" was considered vital to school success, while mental illness was described as "the most serious evil of the time" (Boler 1999). Educators observed then that some children had negative attitudes in school, in part because they did not see schooling supporting their success (financial or otherwise) in the future. In this case, educators saw these attitudes as dysfunctional and in need of intervention: "Either the attitudes must be replaced, or social changes must come about" (Boler 1999: 51). As they saw it, they should change either the economic situation or the attitudes of students to get them to complete school. (They went with the latter.)

In that era, different emotions were regarded as functional for girls and women versus boys and men. Louisa May Alcott recalled learning in school that girls were to develop patience, generosity, perseverance, and denial, and rid themselves of vices of idleness, willfulness, pride, "activity," and "love of cats" (Simons 1990). In contrast, boys were expected to develop bravery, assertiveness, activeness, conviction, and pride (Boler 1999). These gendered expectations were framed as natural and (somewhat paradoxically) as what society needed. Until recently, emotional education has always been gendered in some such way, as the roles of men and women in society have been seen as different in the eyes of major thinkers, from Plato and Socrates in Ancient Greece and Confucius in Ancient China, to Rousseau, in his treatises on the education of Emile and Sophie.

Recently, educational psychologists have focused less on gender and emotions and more on *academic* emotions needed to succeed, regarding these (explicitly or implicitly) as "positive" emotions, such as alertness, curiosity, open-mindedness, patience, and perseverance, in contrast to "negative" emotions, like impatience, anger, frustration, and anxiety. In recent books on emotions in education published by psychologists, these emotions are most often commented on, because they are held as most relevant to school success as conventionally measured (for instance by high-stakes exams) (e.g., Pekrun and Linnenbrink-Garcia 2014).

However, for positive psychologists, positive emotions not directly connected to school (or exam) success, such as happiness, empathy, and gratitude, are also highly valued. For positive psychologists, being functional is about consistently feeling and expressing good emotions. They believe good emotions lead to good behaviors, which benefit the individual and others around them (Seligman 2002). Being happy and grateful will help a person be optimistic and perseverant in the face of challenges. Thus, it will help them not give up or be vulnerable to stress when encountering difficulties, leading them to greater success in life and inspiring them to help others around them.

One of the reasons that psychological views of emotion are influential in education is because they are believed to "work." Psychologists see what they do as based in empirical (social) science. While emotions themselves are not visible, psychologists aim to fix problems related to emotions that they can observe through tracing cause-and-effect relationships (of reported behaviors and experiences) and encouraging people to change their perspectives and/or their behaviors to improve their lives. For instance, educational psychologists understand that (too much) test anxiety can lead to poor test performance, and they therefore aim to help students decrease test anxiety. In this context, teachers and school leaders look to them for solutions. More broadly, it is becoming popular for ordinary people to see a counsellor when they have emotional problems, to enhance their quality of life and their ability to achieve their goals (like I did after my divorce). In this sense, psychology promises solutions.

But fixing problems through psychology can be a double-edged sword. While psychologists can be scientific in their research, enhancing human "functioning" involves making subjective judgments about how people *should* "work." In this case, psychologists can overlook perspectives on "what works" that go beyond the status quo or beyond their own or others' assumptions. In other words, what is functional often gets taken for granted. Yet what is functional is subjective and changes over time. As I mentioned before, it was considered functional until recently that girls and boys should feel and express different emotions based on gender or sex differences. Worse, homosexuality was historically treated as a disorder by psychologists, before enough people in the field realized and admitted (in the 1970s) that it is not in any objective or scientific way unhealthy, wrong, or dysfunctional (Ellis, Riggs, and Peel 2019). Thus, psychologists tend to think about functionality and wellbeing in terms of social norms, without reflecting more deeply on how emotional (and other psychological) matters relate to ethics or morality in society at large.

Today psychologists often think about solutions and functionality in terms of what is sought by those they are aiming to help: what wellbeing means to the individual seeking counselling or the student seeking school success. However, in this case, as is sometimes observed in medicine generally, there can be a tendency, in the promise of solving problems, to focus on symptoms and provide quick and possibly superficial solutions, rather than examining underlying issues. This is partly due to the individual focus in these fields. Thus, doctors may encourage people to eat healthier, but they rarely address a food economy that makes healthy eating more expensive than Kentucky Fried Chicken. Meanwhile, people may not always have their own ultimate best interests in mind. A man may want to lose weight to be more attractive rather than healthier. A principal may be more interested in student exam success than overall wellbeing. Here, careful psychologists will reflectively make value-oriented judgment calls by relating what their patients say to the broader context. But ultimately, they focus on helping individuals in functional terms rather than on the larger picture.

Philosophical Views

There is no singular, widely held philosophical view about emotions. Across traditions, some deny a place for emotions in ethical life or a role for ethics beyond emotions. Others emphasize a connection between emotions and ethics. In this section, I explore some of the range of perspectives on emotions in Western and Eastern thought to give a sense of the complexity and place of emotions in philosophical reflection across contexts. I consider in particular how philosophers relate (or do not relate) emotions to questions of ethics and morality.

Western Views

Do Emotions Have a Role to Play in Ethics?

In some Western philosophies, the answer to this question is basically no. Indeed, many consider Western philosophy a realm where *denials* about the importance of emotions in life have been all too common (Boler 1999; Noddings 1984). Deontology and utilitarianism are two cases in point. *Deontology* explores ethics and morality in terms of rules people can and should follow. Kant developed an approach to morality based on rules everyone could follow. One of his rules was (to paraphrase) that one should not do anything that prevents another person from pursuing her own interests (Kant 1996).

Kant thus favored logical thinking for constructing moral rules. He upheld this stance in "An Answer to the Question: 'What Is Enlightenment?'" (Kant 1970). Here he contrasted methodical, "autonomous" thought with the apparently negative influences of internal fears, "passions," and sentimentality (Jackson 2007). Kant's contemporary legacy can be seen in the writings of Rawls (2000) and Kohlberg (1981), who both argued that the best kind of moral thinking is based upon principles derived from rational judgment, rather than by partial connections to others or emotional considerations. They relatedly observe how emotions such as love, anger, and fear can *cloud* judgment, potentially steering people toward immoral and unethical practices, such as corrupt favoritism to family members and complacency with a non-thinking but emotionally pleasing way of life (Jackson 2021).

One sees the appeal to rationality in Rawls's (1993) thought experiment of the original position. In this position, one uses the "veil of ignorance" to make decisions about what is best for society, by imagining not knowing what their personal position is relative to others (for instance, rich or poor), instead thinking more abstractly about what is best for all (and particularly the worst off). Meanwhile, in moral psychology Kohlberg created several case studies to measure people's development in moral thinking. One of his cases asked people to consider whether it is moral for a man to steal a medicine he cannot pay for to save his wife's life (Kohlberg, Levine, and Hewer 1983). Kohlberg evaluated the merit of people's answers based on the rationales given. Those who appealed in an apparently impartial way to principled and universalizable reasons were seen as more morally developed than those whose answers mentioned emotional, social, or subjective considerations.

Utilitarianism is also based on principles. In this case, the primary rule is that one should do whatever leads to the greatest good for the greater number of people. The trolley problem (Foot 1967) shows the difference this perspective makes. Consider that five people are tied to a train track and about to be killed by an approaching train. It is possible, however, to pull a lever to direct the train to another track, upon which a single person is tied. One thus has the choice to pull the lever, killing one person, or do nothing and allow five people to die. Some will argue against pulling the lever on the grounds that it is wrong to intentionally harm anyone or disturbing to do so. However, utilitarians will see it as preferable to save five lives.

Singer argues that people in wealthy countries should donate more than normally expected to alleviate poverty around the world (2019). Here, a minor personal sacrifice costing as much as a cup of coffee per day can make a big difference in the lives of others, making the trade-off worthwhile. Like Rawls and Kohlberg, Singer is skeptical about appeals to emotions in moral decision making, linking emotion to bias, partiality, and irrationality. As he states, "reasoning may tell you that you ought to be doing something substantial to help the world's poorest people, but your emotions may not move you to act in accordance with this view" (2019: 257).

In relation, Boler's *Feeling Power: Emotions and Education* (1999) traces how *controlling* emotions has been emphasized in the history of Western education. Throughout educational texts over centuries, emotions (particularly anger and related negative emotions) are continuously framed as disruptive influences that students should "master." Today, such approaches can be seen to complement psychological orientations that similarly prioritize emotional self-control (or "mastery") as key to development (Jackson 2021). An emphasis on principles, deliberation, and rationality can also be seen in Hand's *A Theory of Moral Education* (2017), which recommends that students learn rational styles of thinking as part of moral education.

At first glance rules-based ethics like deontology and utilitarianism seem practical, easy to follow, and in line with how we live our lives. We live in societies governed by rules and principles that are (or should be) equally applicable to all and generally beneficial to all. "Thou shalt not kill" and other universal rules are basically agreed upon and believed in by people around the world, whether they call themselves deontologists or Christians or Muslims or atheists, or none of the above. However, these views have been challenged over time.

Some argue that deontologists and utilitarians rely upon emotional kinds of evaluation (Greene 2007, 2013; Greene et al. 2004; Okin 1989), but they ignore it, hide it, or are unaware of or in denial about it. Others question whether emotions *cloud* judgment or *intelligently inform it*, about the most important matters in our lives, like love, family, and relationships (Crittenden 1999). In relation to these concerns, some critique deontologists and utilitarians for being biased about how people normally should think. That is, they illustrate how *some* people think (or how they think that they think), but they ignore or reject diverse contexts and positions, while idealizing capacities to think independently and rationally (Noddings 1984). More specifically, while some Western men like to use (or imagine they are using) rationality, that does not make this type of thinking universally desirable (Gilligan 1982). This response has been given particularly to Kohlberg, whose findings suggested that white men were more developed moral thinkers than women and people of color (and people from other cultures), failing to consider how cultural and social contexts influence moral behavior in everyday life.

Does Ethics Have a Role to Play in Emotions?

On the other hand, some philosophers prioritize emotions over cognitive judgments in thinking about morality and ethics. There are two particularly relevant views here. The first is *emotivism*. Emotivism regards moral statements as reflections of emotion—not as universal ethical rules. Take Ayer's (1936: 107) distinction between matters of fact versus value:

> If I say to someone, "You acted wrongly in stealing that money," I am not stating anything more than if I had simply said, "You stole that money." In adding that this action is wrong .... I am simply evincing my moral disapproval of it. It is as if I had said, "You stole that money," in a peculiar tone of horror. ... If now I generalise ... and say, "Stealing

money is wrong," I produce a sentence that has no factual meaning—that is, expresses no proposition that can be either true or false. ... I am merely expressing certain moral sentiments.

According to emotivism, our sense of approval or disapproval of others' actions is not objective in a way that can be confirmed or rejected through rational thought (see also Russell 1961). Such a view dismisses Kantian and Rawlsian projects of elucidating universal moral laws, reinterpreting their expressions as preferences. Here emotions matter, but they are not seen as guided by rational thought.

Existentialism also takes a skeptical view of universalist ethics in light of subjective experience. Existentialists hold that authenticity and being connected to one's feelings and emotional experiences are vital in life. They also reflect upon an oft-noticed disconnect between how we may feel and the social rules we face related to others' expectations: For instance, a person may believe that she should feel thankful for receiving a kind and thoughtful gift, but for whatever reason (perhaps she is not in a sociable or good mood that day), she does not. Many people believe that such a mismatch between social rules and emotions requires some correction or refinement of the latter. However, for existentialists a correction would amount to a dismissal or rejection of one's spontaneous, authentic feelings. Thus, existentialists question the goodness of the social world and status quo that commonly rejects people's feelings and experiences (Sartre 1943). Camus' *The Stranger* (1988) takes up this idea. The stranger does not follow the rules or expectations of society when expressing himself, but he is in sync with how he personally experiences the world (Roberts 2013).

For existentialists, there are no objectively positive or negative feelings. Instead, so-called negative feelings, of anxiety, fear, and stress, are important parts of being human (Sartre 1943). They therefore reject the idea that certain emotions are more functional or morally apt than others. In the case of an anxious student, an existentialist might argue that their test anxiety is acceptable, "right," and normal. The emotions should not be "fixed" in this case. While psychologists might worry that anxiety could prevent success in examinations, an existentialist reply is that success in life is not necessarily about high marks. On the other hand, another student might *lack* test anxiety from a psychological view. That student would also be "right" according to an existentialist, so long as they are facing (rather than denying) an emotional experience that is authentically their own (Jackson 2021). Among existentialists, courage is thus particularly valued, alongside other emotions that help a person be authentic in light of demands to conform to social expectations.

While many people value authenticity and reject demands for blind conformity to social norms, emotivist and existentialist ideas are not that influential in education or other practical domains beyond philosophical circles. This is (at least partly), because they provide no obvious paths for dealing with social problems or disagreements (Jackson 2021; see also Roberts 2016). Instead, they appear amoral (or morally irrelevant) and relativistic. Instead of guiding or discouraging any action or behavior, these views seem to suggest that anything goes when it comes to emotions (for a more nuanced discussion, see Roberts 2016; Russell 1961). This makes it difficult to justify any particular kind of education about emotions. Yet education of emotions is all around us and surely can be done in better and worse ways (Jackson 2021). Two more palatable approaches when it comes to emotions in life, which seem to evade this binary of prioritizing either emotionality or rationality, are virtue ethics and care ethics.

Integrating Reason and Emotions: Virtue Ethics and Care Ethics

According to Aristotle and others following his lead, virtues are good moral qualities influencing how people behave and treat others. Chief virtues for Aristotle included wisdom, prudence, justice, fortitude (or perseverance), courage, generosity, and temperance. Other lists of virtues in Western thought include the cardinal virtues of prudence, justice, fortitude, and temperance and theological virtues of faith, hope, and charity.

As Aristotle saw it, virtues are "mean states" between excess and deficiency. For instance, to be too courageous is to be brash and foolish, while to be lacking in courage is to be fearful. Practical wisdom (or *phronesis*) is required to consider the situation here. One should not have the same level of courage in every moment of life. It is wise to feel fearful in a risky situation. But being virtuous in this case involves cultivating courage through practical wisdom to face fear (Sreenivasan 2020). In other cases, courage is not required at all, such as when one is considering whether to have a third piece of chocolate cake at breakfast (Curzer 2017). Here, one should learn to sync their feelings with their actions in response to a particular situation with *appropriate* courage, as needed.

Virtue ethicists observe that being virtuous takes hard work. Like others, they recognize that one's emotions are not always well synced to their beliefs and understandings about what is right. For virtue ethicists, education is key here, as we can train and educate children about what they should feel and develop their self-regulation abilities. Virtue ethicists see this as an extension or formalization of what we normally do. Caregivers and teachers repeatedly tell young children to be calm, to say thank you, to feel grateful, and to be caring and generous, when these responses are clearly not natural to children—when children often run around and scream and cry in response to situations that do not align with their desires. Additionally, virtue ethicists regard developing virtue as something one never finishes inside or outside of school, as life always presents new challenges (Miller 2014). Thus, from a virtue ethics view, one can always do better and feel better. Virtue cultivation is never final but, on the other hand, no one is expected to always be perfectly virtuous.

In virtue ethics, as in psychology, emotional development is ultimately seen as a personal task. A person should strive to understand their emotions to achieve their goals (Kristjánsson 2013). This can be seen particularly in the work of the Jubilee Centre for Character and Virtues at the University of Birmingham which has created numerous resources for educators, including lesson plans encouraging students to reflect on their emotions and how they can control and change them (n.d.a):

> Sometimes, when we act before we think, we can act in ways that we may regret and do not show our virtues. It is like our emotions are in control. Before we act, it is good to take a pause to think about how we are feeling and what we want to do next. ...

- Counting to 10 slowly.
- Taking a deep breath.
- Walking away.
- Singing a short song in our heads (e.g., Happy Birthday) before acting.

Thus, virtue ethics shares a key limitation with psychology, in that it focuses primarily on the individual. While virtue ethicists (and psychologists) know that the world has problems and people face unfair challenges, they tend to still encourage people to "work" on themselves rather than external circumstances (Kristjánsson 2018; Jackson 2021). An example of this can be found in Nussbaum's work on anger (2016). In discussing a woman who has learned that her friend has been raped, Nussbaum emphasizes that her task in this situation is to rid herself of anger, as she regards anger as unproductive in responding to any situation (2016). Here, the prioritization of personal development is problematic when it places burdens on individuals to always be calm and collected, as if individual emotions are more important than social problems, such as the pervasiveness of rape and related violence against women (Jackson 2021; see also Tessman 2005). In other words, the problem goes beyond one woman's emotions, yet the woman's calmness (about rape) seems to be Nussbaum's primary concern.

Kristjánsson has discussed this basic challenge in virtue ethics and psychology as a "chicken-or-egg problem" (2013). The problem, as Kristjánsson describes it, is that while responding to both the environment and the individual in a situation may be useful, one must *start somewhere*. In this context, Kristjánsson defends a focus on individuals before situations: "For developmental and pragmatic reasons, it is more feasible to start with the individual child, student or classroom than the whole school system of society" (2013). Additionally, he acknowledges that "care ethicists, who understand the self-goals of emotion education explicitly in terms of improving self-*relations*, may have the strongest weapons in their arsenal" in relation to this issue (2018, p. 175, emphasis in original).

Care ethics is significantly informed by women's experiences, given different expectations and gender roles men and women have faced throughout history. For Noddings, caring is at the heart of human life (1984). As she observes, none of us would be where we are without having been cared for. Thus, appropriate caring behavior and relations are key to becoming a person who can contribute and participate in society. For Noddings and other care ethicists, caring is a practice (i.e., something we *do*), within a relation (one cares *for another*).

Care ethics shares with virtue ethics an appreciation for practical reason, as not all caring relationships are the same. That is, appropriate caring is situational. To care properly requires that one is attentive, responsive, and respectful within a particular relationship and context. In addition, apt caring implies the presence of certain emotions, of empathy, compassion, openness, and attentiveness (Noddings 1984). Care ethicists thus argue that people should develop abilities to care and engage in caring relations through childhood and family experiences and education. In relation, they argue that schools and other institutions should be caring places. Teachers and school leaders should care for students through looking after their wellbeing and development needs, rather than only concerning themselves with academic achievements.

While virtue ethics and care ethics both require the capacity to exercise practical wisdom, virtue ethics has been more concerned with public sphere contexts, where people are framed as equal citizens or individuals, rather than in terms of their relations with and needs for (and dependencies on) others. Furthermore, while love is arguably a cardinal virtue reflecting the value of caring, many virtues more frequently praised in virtue ethics are framed in highly individual terms and as "internal" in nature (such as courage, gratitude, and perseverance), with their interpersonal and community implications less often dwelled upon.

Care ethics can also be seen as a critical rejoinder to deontology and utilitarianism, which care ethicists note fail to consider as part of ethics the importance of caring and women and children's experiences. As care ethicists point out, women are often treated as deficient in research which assumes the superiority of rational deontological views, such as Kohlberg's work (Gilligan 1982). Yet women have *learned* to see relationships as important in their lives, in line with expectations girls and women face to be other-oriented and caring. And it is true that relations of caring are vital in human development, yet somehow seem to go beyond the bounds of philosophical concern for most deontologists (and utilitarianisms, among others).

Care ethics resonates with many educators given its recognition of the importance of social roles, relationships, and contexts to human life and society, as well as the value of whole-person development. Moreover, many see the focus on happy, healthy individuals and communities articulated by care ethicists (and, to a lesser extent, by virtue ethicists) as a refreshing rejoinder to instrumentalist business-as-usual approaches to schooling that focus on achievement, accountability, and performance above all else. That said, care ethics can risk painting an overly rosy, idealistic picture of the nature of caring (Berges 2015; Jackson 2021) and can sometimes appear to overlook unfair expectations for women to dedicate themselves to caregiving work (Jackson 2019a). Furthermore, in comparison with more relationally oriented perspectives such as Confucianism, care ethics still tends to focus more on individual development and individual activities than on the importance of interpersonal relations in life.

Eastern Views

The Western views mentioned here previously represent the tip of the iceberg when it comes to the diversity of philosophical perspectives on emotions and education around the world. To briefly illustrate more about the array of views of emotions found within and across societies, it is worth mentioning how emotions are understood in a few Eastern traditions. Here I consider Confucianism and Buddhism.

Confucius and his followers articulated a very different view of the relationship between emotions, ethics, and good living than major players in the Western world. For Confucians, people always firstly exist in relation to others. And being related to others, in families and other networks, is important for how people are, feel, think, and behave. Starting from this view, emotions are not internal or "inside" people as they are in most Western thought, while emotional development and virtues cultivation cannot be separated from interpersonal connections. Good relationships, rather than good individuals, are prioritized in this understanding. Good relations are harmonious and beneficial to all. But this does not mean that relationships should be "mutually beneficial" in the sense that individuals' benefits are weighed or measured separately from one another (Jackson 2021). The nature of the relationship is more highly valued than what any party "gets out of it."

When it comes to an emotion like gratitude, there is no individual-level way that one should have gratitude, such as always saying thank you in a particular sincere way. The right way to experience and express gratitude depends rather upon *who* you are in relation to *who* gave you a gift, for example, as a parent versus a child or an employer versus an employee. While virtue ethics and care ethics also encourage a critical consideration of the situation in behaving virtuously, the "chicken-or-egg problem" previously mentioned is not an issue here, because one should not prioritize either individuals or situations in Confucian ethics. Rather, because the person is always firstly part of a situation and interpersonal relation, one logically starts with the situation and relation. Thus, there is no individual-level perspective, situation, or norm for behavior that could come first.

As a result of the sustained focus on relations, Confucius and his followers paid attention to what Western thinkers often consider to be trivial matters of social conduct or rituals: dress, manners, ways of communicating, and how people in different social positions ought to perform and behave toward others (Wong and Jackson 2023). While Western philosophers sometimes regard rituals and good manners as less important than other matters from a moral perspective, underneath the focus on politeness, social expectations, and considerateness is a deep appreciation in Confucianism for how one's choices always impact others and shape interpersonal and wider social relations (Sarkissian 2014).

Because of its interest in rules for behavior, some have linked Confucianism with deontology (Liu 2004). Meanwhile, others see more of a link with virtue ethics, given Confucian elaborations on virtues, such as benevolence, righteousness, propriety, wisdom, and fidelity, and the importance of context and practical wisdom (Liu 2004). However, a clearer connection can be made between Confucianism and care ethics (Epley 2015; Li 1994; Wei 2007). In both, relationships are valued as being at the heart of life. However, Confucianism goes further in this regard, more strongly emphasizing how relations, of parents and children and husbands and wives, are foundations for all relationships in society: of youth with elders and citizens with the state (You, Rud, and Hu 2018).

This emphasis on relations has a major impact on Confucian views of emotions. As mentioned in the last chapter, in the case of happiness, Chinese people discuss it less often as a matter of internal feelings. Rather, in China and other Confucian heritage contexts (such as Japan and Korea), happiness is more often defined in relation to participating in a group that is flourishing (Ho, Duan, and Tang 2014). While Western scholars (e.g., Nussbaum 1994) identify a societal need for compassion and empathy, seeing a deep understanding of others' feelings as a *missing* element of social relations in (Western) society, in Confucian heritage contexts empathy and related other-oriented dispositions are regarded as essential for all relationships starting from childhood (Jackson 2021). Thus, what might be thought about as remarkable compassion or empathy for a child in a Western society would not be considered as so exceptional in these contexts, where sensitivity to others at a deep level is commonly expected.

However, many have also noted oppressive possibilities of Confucianism. To put it simply, widely held Confucian values of fidelity and filial piety are illiberal. Children are expected to treat elders with a high level of caring and respect which is not matched by equal recognition and treatment among older people toward younger people. (Some might say there should be *equivalent* recognition, but it is not the "same" or *equal*.) Confucianism has also advocated a special role for women in society—or rather, outside society, at home (Herr 2003; Sarkissian 2014). Additionally, Confucianism has regularly been called upon to support trust in political leaders over democratic principles. Deference, respect, and gratitude for the political elite are often expected and encouraged, while the particular interests of ordinary people in society are framed as less important. In China and Japan, kowtowing is often seen as virtuous, expressing deep deference and indebtedness toward elders and those in power. Such appeals to traditional relations and hierarchies are rarely considered fundamental in more liberal, equality-oriented societies (for example, the United States or United Kingdom).

Confucianism can thus be contrasted with Daoism, another East Asian-based view that is more akin to existentialism in its focus on authenticity and individual experience. Daoist scholars have protested the influence of Confucianism throughout history, arguing that the Confucian obsession with manners, rituals, customs, and appropriate behavior is oppressive and not intrinsically good for all. Daoists have in relation described Confucian teachings regarding civility and filial piety as "forms of self-imprisonment": immoral manipulations that ultimately benefit teachers, elders, and elites, harming people as individuals for the sake of an abstract sense of community (Sarkissian 2014). Similar to existentialism, Daoism does not emphasize social rules or any kind of global or general sense of ethics, due to its appreciation for subjectivity, individuality, and authenticity (Maki 2018). However, it continues to be attractive as a counterpoint to a more prescriptive Confucian view.

In contrast to Confucianism, there is no singular *Buddhist* approach to emotions basically taken by Buddhists around the world, from India to Japan and the United States. One well-known approach holds that Buddhists should be unemotional and pacifistic—similar to the Stoics (Kupperman 1995). The Four Noble Truths in Buddhism stress overcoming suffering, desire, and attachment, letting go, and nirvana as the cessation of yearning and craving. Here, restraint and emotional control, or perhaps even emotional eradication, seem fundamental (Jackson 2021).

However, another Buddhist orientation emphasizes positive, sociable emotions, of mindfulness, loving kindness, and compassion (McRae 2012, 2015, 2017). Numerous other virtues that kindle emotions are also commended in many Buddhist teachings, such as generosity, wisdom, energy, patience, honesty, goodwill, and determination—as are means of actively developing virtues via "inner" peace and self-cultivation, such as meditation. In relation, many have noted similarities of Buddhism with virtue ethics (and, to a lesser extent, psychological views of emotions), as each encourages people to look "within" and develop emotional awareness and self-control (McRae 2015).

In this context, the role of emotions in ethical action can be debated in Buddhism. Consider anger. Some take for granted that the dissolution of anger is key to Buddhism. Here, they look to the Dalai Lama as a model, who has spoken of facing harms caused to him and Tibet by the Chinese government with patience and gratitude (Fitzgerald 1998). Those following his view tend to hold anger as unhelpful and undesirable. On the other hand, Thich Nhat Hanh valued anger as useful and productive, likening it to compost in a garden (2001; Yancy and hooks 2015). Similarly, other Buddhist ethicists discuss the "purification" of anger, to "distil" and understand anger and the best ways to manage or use it in support of good actions (McRae 2015). There are also debates among Buddhists about whether mindfulness and meditation have a critical moral and ethical quality and aim or are entirely amoral dispositions and activities, primarily involving passive acceptance of oneself in the world (Jackson 2021).

Thus, a Buddhist education could encourage one to develop positive emotions, to engage the spectrum of emotions, to critically consider emotion's role in human life, to focus on emotional release, or to develop a more stony or passive experience, depending on the particular view of Buddhism taken. Furthermore, there has been much reflection and debate about techniques of Buddhist meditation and related forms of emotional control and release within psychological and virtue ethics approaches, although they do not necessarily convey the spectrum of Buddhist orientations (Hyland 2015; Jackson 2021). As we will see in later chapters, it is therefore interesting to consider *which* Buddhist views get taken up and how in education, as there is sometimes a risk of cherry-picking Buddhist views one prefers and stereotyping all of Buddhism accordingly, ignoring the diversity found in this tradition.

The Inward Turns and the Politics of Emotions

As discussed here, common views of emotions, particularly in Western societies, tend to approach emotions in an individual way. Emotions are seen as something people *have*, that are *inside* them, that can be "fixed" through individual practices. This understanding of emotional wellbeing can be described as the "inward turn," as individuals are encouraged to adapt their emotions to accord with expectations of others around them, to be a good student or employee. In this context, the *politics of emotions* (Ahmed 2004a; Jackson 2021) questions how social and political processes influence expectations about emotions in ways that are not always fair, just, or equal. While this view does not focus on morality or ethics as conceived in Western philosophy, it provides a critical response to some of the blind spots of the inward turn.

Marxist, Foucauldian, and feminist theories undergird the politics of emotions view (Jackson 2021). Marx noted how private businesses shape people's desires and values in ways that can run counter to their wellbeing. Today, people crave iPhones and designer clothes and accessories. These desires are not "natural." iPhone and Gucci handbags do not intrinsically benefit people. Furthermore, the specific goods may not last (or be valuable) for more than a few years. Yet advertisers create these and other desires that encourage people to shop endlessly. At the same time, Marx (and Weber 1959) noted how religion (particularly Christianity) encourages people to value hard work and feel good about working hard—attitudes which can benefit businesses as much, if not more than, ordinary people.

Foucault was influenced by Marx and Weber as he developed a critique of "care of the self" as a focus on self-maintenance encouraged by external parties—religious and political authorities—but practiced by individuals (1979). Foucault observed how the cultivation of "confessional" habits and forms of reporting of one's thoughts and feelings to others, from priests to therapists and teachers, serves as a means for elite social interests to be individualized and taken up by ordinary people. In relation, Foucault's concept of "biopolitics" illustrates how the wellbeing of people as mass populations is valued by politicians as vital to political economic aspects of managing a country (1984). In this case, those higher up in society shape expectations about what it means to be healthy or well in ways that benefit themselves as much as those "beneath" them. They thus encourage people to internalize their views, based on a picture of the wellbeing or functioning of society as a whole, to perform "self-care" and monitor themselves according to top-down, socioeconomic visions of flourishing.

In prisons and in schools, people are required or encouraged to "confess" their feelings and dispositions, which are framed in policy discourse as a matter of community interest. These practices teach people to "police" their inner experiences over time. For example, after a lesson where students are asked to report how they feel in front of the classroom, students will become more mindful and aware about how they feel in the future, gradually aspiring to have and be able to report feelings that seem desirable to their teacher and peers—for example, to be in a good mood in class, rather than a bad mood.

Other elaborations of the politics of emotions come from feminist theorizing. Hochschild's *The Managed Heart* (1983) observed how some professions—particularly "caring" and service jobs often held by women—involve "emotional labor." In her text, she notes how women flight attendants are expected to perform pleasing emotions for air travelers. In relation, they are evaluated by their employers based on their ability to smile and appear calm and happy, to act like loving, caring girlfriends or mothers to passengers (especially men), as this is regarded as an effective way to manage flight safety and other air travel requirements. Here, Hochschild notes how difficult this work can be. In their efforts to constantly perform pleasant emotions, flight attendants experience alienation from what they really feel: for example, stressed, tired, or irritated. In this context, their smiles begin to clash with their true feelings, leading to frustration, exhaustion, and emotional disconnectedness.

Inspired by Hochschild, Ahmed (2010) explores how boys and men are encouraged to be assertive, competitive, confident, and adventurous, while girls and women are expected to be kind, caring, happy, domestic, and humble. Today, parents and teachers treat boys and girls differently in subtle ways, impacting how they learn emotions based on gender (Jackson 2019a). Women and girls who deviate from mainstream scripts, who do not act polite, attentive, happy, and patient, are considered "killjoys" who fail to match social expectations and thereby displease others (Ahmed 2010). In this context, while boys and men are allowed to express anger or frustration about everyday problems, it is treated as a negative experience for the whole group if girls or women express such emotions, leading girls and women to experience more emotional alienation as they relate to the world around them.

Emotional expectations also differ according to race and ethnicity. Ahmed describes in Britain the "melancholy migrant"—a Muslim or Sikh Asian immigrant—who is seen as failing to fit in and adapt due to his or her different appearance or behavior (2010). While Britain identifies as a liberal democratic society where people are free to practice their beliefs and follow their cultural traditions equally, much public attention has been paid to minority religious and ethnic groups as unhappy and therefore unsuccessful in society. Their (apparently bad) attitudes and (apparent lack of) success are thus associated with their choosing to preserve their ways of life—rather than, for instance, their experiencing misrecognition, intolerance, prejudice, and discrimination (Ahmed 2010; Jackson 2019a).

In US education, Black children and adults are targeted more often for disciplinary interventions, punishment, detention, and imprisonment in educational and criminal justice/corrections systems due to what is perceived in a white-oriented and white-dominated society as their unacceptably unruly, uncivil, or threatening behavior (Gay 2016; Wingfield 2007). This unjust treatment harkens back to a time when white supremacy largely went unquestioned in the society and white people routinely regarded people of color as uncivilized, inferior, and deficient. Today, a double standard in interpretating people's emotional expressions based on race tracing this history remains. In an organized political protest, a loud and impatient Black man or woman may be framed as rude, irrational, angry, and threatening, even when they do the same things as white counterparts (Gay 2016; Zerilli 2014).

More broadly, happiness, patience, gratitude, and other positive emotions are increasingly promoted by political and educational leaders, in part because they help maintain economically productive, politically stable societies and "well-behaved" classrooms (Boler 1999; Ecclestone 2012). Sometimes people should not be happy or patient, however, and there can be benefits, for example, to being angry. When experiencing racism, sexism, or other social ills, one has good reason to become angry, indignant, or impatient (Ahmed 2004a). On the other hand, happiness and gratitude are *not always* healthy in all situations. Yet political and educational leaders ignore such complexity by prioritizing stability, order, and productivity above all else, failing to consider potentially harmful tradeoffs in this domain.

Thus, political understandings of emotions showcase how diverse emotional experiences can be squashed by simplified perspectives on wellbeing. First, positive psychologists (among others) paint a picture of emotional intelligence and socioemotional learning wherein it is normal to identify and regulate one's emotions. However, in reality not everyone finds this easy all of the time (or most of the time). In this case, people are pressured to *perform* emotional identification and regulation, regardless of what they really feel (Boler 1999; Jackson 2021). This can lead to unhealthy emotional suppression and a sense of disconnection. Minorities within a society are also susceptible here to risks around emotional double standards in expectations.

Second, emotional experiences and expressions vary around the world. As mentioned in the first chapter, service with a smile does not make sense in Hong Kong as it does in the United States. In white Western-oriented schools and universities, Chinese and other Asian students (among others) are often held as suspect, as culturally deficient or not confident, assertive, or honest enough, due to deferent behaviors they have learned in the past, such as speaking only when spoken to, limiting eye contact with authority figures, maintaining a distance from authority figures, and acting serious (Jackson 2021). Likewise, a United States born-and-raised child enrolling in a local school in East Asia for the first time is also not likely to follow or understand expectations around their emotional performances, as they have also learned something different (for example, to be active, assertive, or funny), which becomes deficient across cultures when people fail to recognize emotional diversity. Thus, the politics of emotions illuminates how universalistic norms harm minorities when those in power assume there is one major way to act, feel, and express emotions.

Recognizing the politics of emotions requires that we think about ethics in education beyond formal principles and abstract values and focus more on how individuals and groups experience the same situations in contrasting ways. As such, this is a more sociological (than philosophical) orientation, focused on on-the-ground realities over idealistic discourses. However, as mentioned earlier, some are critical of shifting attention from the individual to society, regarding it as more pragmatic to focus on the individual and as radical or reactionary to focus on social conditions (Kristjánsson 2013). Nonetheless, from a broad view, "mental hygiene," "conflict resolution," and socioemotional learning have been evolving for a long time, and it is not actually clear whether they are pragmatically achieving their major expressed aim (i.e., helping wellbeing) or its opposite. We will see how these perspectives play out more in education in the chapters that follow.

Conclusion

This chapter gave a whirlwind tour of how emotions are seen from different disciplinary, cultural, and theoretical starting points. Its task was to highlight a diversity of perspectives which can be seen to clash with each other (and complement each other in some cases), in place of any singular view of emotions. While psychological (particularly positive psychology) and virtue ethics views are popular, they have limitations, as we have seen here. This chapter has thus aimed to pave the way for a more focused discussion of different approaches to emotions in education. In the next chapter, I focus on some specific emotions to consider the importance of these views in school settings.

CHAPTER THREE

Educating Emotions: Accentuate the Positive?

Around the world, teachers are increasingly tasked with supporting student emotional wellbeing (especially in early years). However, they may or may not be given specific guidance on how to do so. Whether we call it socioemotional learning, therapeutic education, or character education, there are rarely set curriculum guidelines or textbooks for how to educate emotions. Meanwhile, the basic facts about what emotions are and why they matter are still up for debate. In this context, many educators may have some flexibility to be creative and critical when it comes to educating for and about emotions. And if they need advice or support, there are all kinds of resources and recommendations available. But how do we evaluate which practices are better or worse? This chapter and the next aim to think through how to answer this kind of question in real-world educational situations. At the same time, they reflect more on *why* we want to help students with emotional development and wellbeing.

This chapter explores how emotions are thought about and taught about in education. In particular, it focuses on how some key emotions have been encouraged. These I have discussed previously as positive emotions. Here, I focus on happiness, compassion, empathy, caring, and gratitude. Many assume that these are good and functional emotions, positively influencing student wellbeing and academic and life success. However, as I will show here, there can also be risks and challenges involved in educating them. These relate to debates about what these emotions are and their benefits in personal and social life. In connection, I explore here how it is important to think through the different ways that the education of emotions can be experienced in real life, as opposed to in ideal or universalized circumstances. Overall, these considerations complicate the picture when it comes to educating so-called positive emotions.

Happiness

In Western society in particular, many see happiness as a worthy goal of schooling. Nussbaum (2012) and Noddings (2003) have both argued for happiness in education. However, their definitions of happiness vary. Nussbaum recommends a moral sense of happiness following a virtue ethics view, describing happiness as a subjective emotional quality combined with moral judgment or evaluation. Just feeling good is not enough for Nussbaum. As she writes, "if I ever notice myself feeling feelings of satisfaction, I blame myself and think that, insofar as I have those I'm like Mill's 'pig satisfied' or Aristotle's 'dumb grazing animals,' and thus, reflectively, I report dissatisfaction with my life as a whole" (2012 : 345).

Noddings, on the other hand, defends happiness in a moral sense and as a good feeling. Such happiness has intrinsic and extrinsic value for Noddings. For instance, she writes, "Happy individuals are rarely violent or intentionally cruel, either to other human beings or to nonhuman animals" (2003: 2), justifying education for happiness in relation to its prosocial benefits. Noddings also argues pragmatically that basic experiences of pleasure, fun, and playfulness help students pay attention and feel satisfied, leading to their more meaningful engagement in school and greater overall wellbeing (2003). In education, Noddings thus calls for more play, games, leisure, and recreation, given the increase over time in structured extracurricular activities, high-stakes testing, formal curricula, and related pressures (2003).

Despite their differences, both Nussbaum and Noddings argue that education should help students feel joy and pleasure as part of their development and what it means to be a good, flourishing person. Psychologists similarly commend happiness, associating it with life satisfaction, flourishing and moral development, and subjective wellbeing (Frey 2008). Positive psychologists emphasize that happiness helps a person achieve their goals, and that happiness, wellbeing, fulfilment, and optimism boost each other and other good traits like altruism and compassion. Seligman (2002) thus recommends that people seek happiness by pursuing pleasant emotions, gratifying experiences, meaningful relationships, and worthwhile achievements.

Education for happiness often involves emotional literacy as a central component (Boler 1999; Bywater and Sharples 2012). Lessons aim to help students recognize and control their emotions, avoid problematic, so-called negative emotions, and cultivate positive emotions. Students in this context learn to see their feelings as part of their personal and educational responsibilities. One example is the School Speciality (2018) Premier Esteem curriculum planner. This handbook asks students to identify what makes them happy with the statement, "Your feelings can change your actions. Know why you feel the way you do. This will help you make good choices" (ES-7). Another lesson encourages students to reflect on their strengths and the strengths of their peers, before discussing "whether this activity made them happier" (Boniwell n.d.). Another approach involves students marking on a scale in front of class how happy (or unhappy) they feel (Boler 1999).

However, there are risks involved with these kinds of lessons and with simplistically promoting happiness in general. First, cultivating, experiencing, and expressing happiness are not always morally good. Many assume that happiness benefits oneself and others (recall Noddings: happy people are rarely violent or cruel). But as an empirical statement, this is not always true. While studies show correlations between happiness, wellbeing, generosity, optimism, and kindness (Kesebir and Diener 2014; Veenhoven 2008), a person can be happy and selfish and unkind. Bentall observes that happier people tend to be more careless, impulsive, and unpredictable (1992: 94). Happiness can lead to eating and drinking alcohol more indulgently, having difficulty with "mundane but essential tasks," and being unrealistic about challenges (1992: 97). Happiness can involve compartmentalizing and avoiding issues that might make a person unhappy or require critical judgments.

More broadly, the world has its problems, and we all have our challenges. Focusing on these to some extent is necessary if we want to experience, participate in, and work to improve the world around us. Alloy and Abramson (1988) defend "depressive realism" as a more negative mindset than what is usually encouraged, which is more attuned to reality, observing how being realistic about the world can be discouraged when carefree optimism is prized over all else. In this context, educators may be challenged to present a curriculum that focuses on (for example) injustice, global climate change, or poverty, as exploring such topics is not likely to directly or immediately (if at all) increase student happiness.

Thus, there is a tension between curricula for feeling good versus curricula for making a difference. This can put educators in a difficult place when demands for education for happiness go too far. As Roberts notes (2016), a dark implication here is that for some teachers, "the goal is to keep students or viewers happy; discomfort should be avoided wherever possible. And where this breaks down, and students or viewers become bored, or restless, or angry, those who provide the teaching or the programming are punished with lower ratings and, where necessary appropriate disciplinary action" (104–5).

Furthermore, there are times students should not be happy or pleased with themselves. As Cigman writes, "the Social and Emotional Aspects of Learning programme teaches children to reach positive conclusions about themselves, saying things like 'I accept myself for who and what I am'. But a child who has just bulled another child should not necessarily be encouraged to say this; it could reinforce a dangerous arrogance or conceit" (2012: 453). While few teachers would intentionally aim to encourage children to feel pleased about bullying others, prioritizing happiness as an individual experience and separating it from moral reflection could have this effect, if students are rewarded for happiness regardless of the context. In relation, activities that focus on students' strengths to feel happy should be balanced with some level of concern with normal human weaknesses and the value of self-improvement. Yet the implication here is that a focus on weaknesses is less worthwhile, as it will not lead to students immediately feeling happy.

There are other noteworthy challenges and limitations in teaching for happiness. In real life, happiness can be fleeting, dynamic, and shifting (Noddings 2003). For most of us, there are times when we think we should feel happy, but we do not, and days that we feel happier than others for no decipherable reason. This is normal and not necessarily unhealthy. Meanwhile, youth life, like adult life, is not always as pleasant and joyous as many people would like to imagine. In this context, students exposed to simple lessons promoting and encouraging happiness may feel guilty or wrong about the dynamic, fleeting nature of their emotions.

In some cases, educators teach, explicitly or implicitly, that students should always be happy, or should always be happy in a given situation: "We should be happy it is such a nice day outside"; "You should be happy that you all received high grades on the exam." Such lessons (formal and informal) are well intended, and most educators do not wish to suggest that anyone should be completely happy all of the time. But because of teacher desires for student happiness (and student desires to please their educators), students can learn from such lessons, ironically, to feel bad about not being happy. Thus, some students can "learn" that something is wrong with them if they are not always (or usually) happy, which can make them feel even worse (Boler 1999).

Such experiences can have long-lasting impacts on some students and their relations with peers and educators. Boler (1999: 101) gives an example of what can happen when a student reports in a lesson that she is not feeling happy:

> The next girl ranks herself at—5 (and indeed in my estimation "looked" very sad). The teacher responds to this, "What do we need to know, class?" Before any student had the opportunity to respond, and without asking the girl herself what she needed or wanted, the teacher answered her own question: "We want to give her space rather than tease her."

As Boler reflects here, this is an arbitrary, potentially harmful conclusion (1999). Why not ask the student what she needs? She may be dealing with a real crisis, which is likely better addressed through an intervention than by isolation. The student may feel physically unwell; she may have problems at home. But often lessons *for* happiness do not encourage active reflection on real-world struggles. In this case, this student may face worse problems and more negative emotional experiences over time, if her challenges are ignored and her teacher encourages her isolation, regarding her negative emotions as taboo.

Such lessons can also lead to other students "learning" that they better be happy—or else. In happiness lessons as in a broader cultural context where people are generally encouraged to be happy (Ehenreich 2009), some will "fake it" to get by. This is indirectly encouraged by lessons which stigmatize happiness "deficiencies" as well as discourses that recommend compartmentalizing (putting aside) challenges and problems: "Sure, you do not feel good—but just look on the bright side. Move on."

All of us have struggled with pressures to compartmentalize or "move on" before, and all of us have worked at times to "grin and bear it." For example, after participating in a depressing meeting focused on a student failure case, you run into a colleague that you have not seen for many months in the hall. In this case, it may be worthwhile not to "dump" on your colleague and complain about the difficult case when they casually ask how you are doing. And you may find that switching gears and chatting cheerfully with your colleague indeed help you move on from the earlier conversations, as you go on to other tasks of the day.

So yes, we can "fake it 'til you make it." However, as a general strategy for dealing with a variety of situations, this can be a dangerous lesson to impart in the context of the classroom. This solution does not help solve real-world problems. Worse, encouraging "fake it 'til you make it" can lead some people to develop unhealthy emotional suppression habits, making it harder for them to improve their lives and feel happy in a meaningful way in the long run (Sarkissian 2014).

This can particularly be a problem for girls and women. As Ahmed (2010) has traced, the message that girls and women must normally exude happiness has often been expressed in Western philosophy. For instance, in *Emile*, Rousseau encourages a girl, Sophie, to seek happiness through marriage: "A good girl finds her happiness in the happiness of a good man" (1979). However, the boy Emile is not encouraged to devote himself in a similar way to his partner or family's happiness (Ahmed 2010). There is no parallel emphasis on Emile's happiness as critical to those around him.

Today girls and women are still encouraged to find happiness within themselves to be pleasing to others. Girls and women (particularly in Western societies) are sometimes asked by family, friends, acquaintances, and strangers on the street to "just smile" rather than express other feelings, such as irritation or sadness or "resting bitch face": the term for the expressions of women who may not be particularly unhappy, but who could still apparently stand to look more chipper (Jackson 2019a). Many women have commented how frustrating such expectations are when sometimes you have a bad day, and when the experience of strangers telling you how to feel (or to "just smile") rarely has the desired outcome (Jackson 2019a).

Finally, it is worth recalling our discussion in the first chapter on McDonald's service "with a smile" and how happiness can look different and be valued differently across cultures. This means that even simple lessons which encourage children to label emojis or themselves or other students with wide-mouthed smiles as "happy" (for example, rather than "goofy" or "silly") might not be entirely effective in diverse classrooms. And a perfectly happy British Chinese student, whose smiling, crinkly eyes would be admired for emanating sincere joy back in Taiwan (e.g., Mai et al. 2011), could become alienated in a classroom where the teacher only recognizes wide-mouthed smiles and therefore sees him in a stereotypical way, as overly serious and joyless, failing to recognize his expression of happiness.

Happiness is valuable in education, and it can be increased (sometimes) through interventions. As Noddings notes, education should not lead to unnecessary suffering (2003). However, negative effects of inadvertently pressuring students to always or normally be happy and express happiness in particular ways often get overlooked in simplified informal and formal curricula for happiness. Meanwhile, lessons that suggest that one should always be happy with themselves and the world around them can be wrong headed. Here a more critical happiness curriculum is feasible, which teaches that happiness is a complex emotion, experienced in different ways across cultures and situations. Thus, the key is to not pursue the educational aim of happiness in an overzealous way, but to consider the aim, intent, and implications of education for happiness more critically overall.

Compassion, Empathy, and Caring

Compassion, empathy, and caring are valued around the world. Understanding and feeling connected to others' emotions (empathy) and positively influenced by others' perspectives (compassion) have often been held as key to being a good person, benefitting others, developing positive relations, and engaging in caring and altruistic acts (Blum 1980; Nussbaum 2001). As discussed previously, Confucianism also holds that developing relations of care for and attention to others is vital. Such accounts are echoed in psychology (e.g., Graham and Taylor 2014). Nussbaum (2001, 2013) and Noddings (1984, 2002) are again proponents for educating for compassion and care.

A major rationale for educating for compassion, empathy, and caring stems from a commonly observed challenge: people often struggle to develop compassion or empathy toward people they see as "different." They struggle to identify with people who they do not recognize as similar to themselves, such as people coming from different ethnic, racial, religious, national, linguistic, and socioeconomic groups (Nussbaum 2001). Across lines of difference, people are also less able to imagine that others are in situations they could someday find themselves in, which is one common motivation for compassion and care. Adam Smith (1969) noted that the average European man would lose more sleep over the loss of his finger than over an earthquake in China killing hundreds (Jackson 2021). Similarly, Nussbaum has observed that one may feel more strongly toward a friend stuck in traffic than a homeless person (2001). Such failures to empathize across difference can decrease the likelihood of compassionate, caring behavior.

Thus, compassion, empathy, and caring are often highlighted in socioemotional learning and character education lessons which encourage the ability to recognize, understand, and interpret others' emotions and perspectives (Brackett and Rivers 2014). Nussbaum recommends (2001, 2013) that students develop empathy and compassion through reading literature which is written by and describes the experiences of people from different backgrounds. She believes this will help cultivate students' sense of connection and motivate them to feel more concerned about and related to others who they may otherwise see as different.

Another recommendation for caring for others across difference is participating in service learning and international exchange trips. Noddings (1984) writes in favor of this approach, noting that "wherever students might be assigned—to hospitals, nursing homes, animal shelters, parks, botanical gardens—a definite expectation would be that their work be a true apprenticeship in caring" (2–3). International exchanges and study experiences are commonly used for students to reflect on their lives in comparison with others (Nesterova and Jackson 2016). Often there is a focus on students understanding and seeing first-hand the struggles others face to develop empathy and compassion.

Others advocate the use of direct instruction on the benefits and how-to of these qualities. The Jubilee Centre encourages students to think about when and how they can and should be compassionate in relation to others. Here, they recommend Buddhist loving kindness meditation (Jubilee n.d.b: 7).

In the first stage, you feel metta [love] for yourself. You start by becoming aware of yourself, and focusing on feelings of peace, calm, and tranquility. You can use an image, like golden light flooding your body. In the second stage you think of a good friend. Bring them to mind as vividly as you can, and think of their good qualities. Feel your connection with your friend, and your liking for them, and encourage these to grow by wishing them well. If it is helpful, you can use an image such as shining light from your heart into theirs. Then think of someone you do not particularly like or dislike. Your feelings towards this person are "neutral". This may be someone you do not know well but see around, such as your postman or someone who regularly serves you in a shop. Include them in your feelings of metta. Then think of someone you are currently having difficulties with. Trying not to get caught up in any difficult feelings, you think of them positively and send your metta to them as well.

The Jubilee Centre relatedly provides lessons so students can learn that "without caring, people would get sick and there would be no-one to help them get better" (n.d.b). Noddings also recommends teaching students directly about caring (2002). Furthermore, she argues that teachers should see their own task as one of caring (and modeling caring).

However, there are some problems with these orientations and approaches. Firstly, empathy, compassion, and care, like happiness, are not always moral qualities. From a philosophical perspective, one can questionx *who* one feels empathy or compassion or caring for, *why*, and *how*. Regarding *who*: For Aristotle there was no virtue in feeling sorry for a person who faced a painful or challenging experience which they deserved (1984). As he indicated, "no good person would be distressed when parricides and bloodthirsty murderers meet punishment." As previously alluded to, one must exercise practical wisdom about *who* in order for their empathy or compassion to be moral.

As for *why*: While empathy, compassion, and care can lead to altruism, they can also be used for personal gain and exploitation of others. Thus, they are not always intrinsically good. "Tactical empathy" is empathy used to manipulate others. Across societies, "poker players, police profilers, military strategists, con artists, Internet scammers, method actors, and everyday romantic Casanovas" understand others' feelings for self-serving rather than altruistic purposes (Hollan 2017: 347). While such uses and abuses of empathy and compassion are better understood across cultures—for example, in Asian contexts (including Confucian heritage settings) where the instrumental aspects of empathy are more clearly recognized— such perspectives in Western societies remain "under-reported and under-studied because of the assumption … that empathy is inherently virtuous" (Hollan 2017: 347).

And in terms of *how*: Problems can occur when one has *too much* empathy and compassion. In "egoism-altruism," one has such strong feelings for others that the conception of self and other is blurred (Cialdini et al. 1997). Selflessness is a moral ideal often invoked in religious traditions, such as Christianity and Buddhism. However, it can be harmful in some cases to feel too much for others without having enough respect for oneself and one's own agency and needs (May 2017). Consider the loving kindness meditation introduced previously. As the meditation focuses more on an internal attitude than on outward responses, some might gather from such a lesson that they should tolerate and accept mistreatment from others to maintain a positive attitude toward them. This could lead to more negative and harmful relationships and situations down the line.

While advocating for care, Noddings also specifies how caring can be appropriate or inappropriate in particular situations. In her care ethics, care must be responsive to others in moral ways: respectful of others and attentive to their needs (Noddings 1984). In this context, not all relations of care are positively experienced by caregivers or those being cared for (Berges 2015). This is important to reflect upon as we consider learning about caring in schools, as young people may face mixed, possibly negative experiences of care at home (Jackson 2021). They may experience caring by unhealthy caregivers who care for them inappropriately: for example, engaging in physically or emotionally abusive behaviors, with wrongheaded beliefs such as that you "spare the rod and spoil the child." In such contexts, to praise and commend care above all else can teach that caregiving should never be questioned. While this notion deviates from Noddings' arguments, one can imagine well-intended educators putting forward the message that all relations of care are good, without realizing the harm it can do in the real world where, unfortunately, not every child experiences healthy caregiving at home.

Meanwhile, given all the problems of the world, demands for care and compassion in society can sometimes feel excessive and become overwhelming for some people. Compassion fatigue, over-functioning, empathy overload, and other dysfunctional experiences occur when people care too much (Jackson 2021). In relation to these challenges, organizations such as Oxfam exploit people whose feelings of empathy and compassion and belief in caring motivate them to donate and volunteer (Jackson 2014a). This might not seem terrible at first glance. However, in the context of ubiquitous demands to "give back," empathy is "a limited resource that we need to use wisely" (Leighton 2011: 226).

Girls and women are particularly vulnerable to compassion fatigue and empathy overload, as in many cases they are encouraged to see themselves firstly as caregivers rather than as people who also deserve to be cared for, thus ignoring their own needs (Houston 1990). While many treat girls and women's caring as a natural, biological phenomenon, apparently backed up by research showing that girls and women value caring more, that girls and women are *expected* to be caring plays a role here (Derntl et al. 2010: 79). On the other hand, discourse which emphasizes girls' and women's capacities and importance in caregiving dismisses the potential desires of and benefits for boys and men to also be empathetic, compassionate, and caring. Instead, boys are often mocked for being caring. This exacerbates gendered expectations while harming boys' and men's wellbeing (Jackson 2021).

Finally, in education strategies encouraged for developing empathy, compassion, and caring have had mixed impacts. While many have advocated students reading multicultural literature to develop empathy, Boler has found that such interventions often result in the cultivation of a kind of *passive* empathy, where students see and technically understand unjust and needless suffering in others' lives, yet fail to develop substantial concern about it (1999). Worse, in some cases reading multicultural literature can result in students merely feeling better about their own place in the world. They may also "learn" that they are becoming better people simply by reading about others' suffering, as this is suggested by some educators and curricula (Boler 1999).

Service learning and international exchange programs which aim to develop compassion and empathy rarely measure students' development of these capacities in a systematic way—or whether student actually help at all in disadvantaged communities (Cook 2012; Nesterova and Jackson 2016). Instead, students can learn in these contexts to see themselves as do-gooders, reflecting power dynamics wherein people in so-called developing countries and other disadvantaged contexts are framed as powerless victims that depend upon the charity and moral goodness of more advantaged people to "show them the light." Here, students may feel they have learned profound lessons about helping others, but they may fail to understand their own role in unjust situations and how the world is experienced by diverse others (Jackson 2021).

Given these challenges, a deeper approach to encouraging empathy circles back to students focusing more critically on suffering in the world (Boler 1999; Zembylas 2008). Yet in real-life applications of this approach, some students quickly feel powerless or hopelessly and anxiously guilty when dwelling upon challenges beyond the scope of what they as individuals can improve. Students may feel distressed, anxious, or traumatized to deeply recognize others' suffering, in a way that leads them to feel paralyzed in relation to making a difference (Jackson 2021). This may lead over time to their cultivating a disposition that is averse to facing diverse others in relation to the discomfort of such experiences (Jackson 2021). These outcomes are not uncommon in international and other service-learning projects where young people learn about the complexity of social problems and how difficult it is to make a difference (Jackson 2013).

Meanwhile, some question the moral undergirdings of students (among others) *wanting* to make a difference as a response to feeling compassion and empathy toward others. Confronted with the tragic situations of others, students often express that they want to "do something" (Hytten and Warren 2003), and many lessons suggest that they should. However, whether this desire to do good is primarily based in an interest to improve their own feelings (for instance of guilt) or the circumstances of others can be unclear. Some argue that since the desire to "do something" is a response to their own experience (or the expectations of others), the desire is inherently self-serving (Hytten and Warren 2003). In any case, a response *to their own discomfort* is not likely to lead to their making a real difference in the lives of others. More generally, given the difficulties in understanding and appropriately responding to the problems of others, as well as cultural differences in how caring and related dispositions and behaviors are experienced and expressed across societies (Kang 2006; Jackson 2021), the assumption that emotions of compassion and empathy can and should guide moral behavior across lines of difference is worth scrutinizing.

As mentioned in the last chapter, many have in contrast encouraged *caution* in responding to emotions such as compassion and empathy in everyday life. The Stoics advocated that people *avoid* acting on emotional responses or personal attachments to others, observing the irrational and unethical possibilities of devoting oneself in a partial way to others (Jackson 2019b). While some associate Buddhism with selfless caring and compassion, others liken it to such Stoicism, as many Buddhists also recognize a dark side to pursuing emotional attachments to others and the need to see interpersonal relations from a broad view (Kupperman 1995). Likewise, while empathy and care toward members of one's community were (and continue to be) valued in Confucian-influenced China, Mozi warned that such care could go too far, enabling corruption when people were only concerned about their personal connections and not with larger matters of justice (Dubs 1951).

Kant (Jackson 2017a), Rawls (2000), and Nagel (1970) have also argued for a more rational approach to altruism, seeing any actions based on emotions as potentially harmful (cf., Blum 1980). Empirical research about altruism in real life backs up the perspective that emotions of empathy and compassion are not always essential to being a good person (Jackson 2021). For instance, in interviews with German rescuers of Jews in Nazi Europe, many expressed being more motivated by a sense of injustice than by feelings of interpersonal connection or the sense that they could someday experience a similar situation (Konarzewski 1992; Monroe 1996).

Thus, we need to ask rather than assume why compassion, empathy, and care are important and what role they play in moral life. Obviously, a world without caring, empathy, and compassion would be bleak. These qualities add to the richness and meaningfulness of life. They contribute to happiness and the depth of a variety of emotional experiences related to connecting with others in a complex, often tragic world. So the point here is not to discard these emotions in education. Rather, the aim should be to cultivate spaces that enable students to appreciate these emotions while also critically understanding the complex moral grammar surrounding their development and expression in connection with diverse others. Compassion, empathy, and caring can be lovely emotional experiences, but ideal examples can obscure complicated realities where they can lead people astray, harm one's sense of self and agency, and encourage a selfless other-orientation lacking critical reflection. It is worth educating about these emotions, but with (appropriate) care.

Gratitude

Traditionally gratitude has been understood as feelings and expressions of thankfulness to others for gifts received. Although some of the ways that it is expressed and experienced vary across societies, this basic sense of gratitude is broadly valued and expected around the world. Most people recognize it as good and right to thank others for gifts and feel grateful. However, another definition has become popular over time, particularly among psychologists. According to this second definition, gratitude can be a kind of appreciation about various aspects of one's life, such as to live in a kind community, an orderly society, or a beautiful world, on a sunny day (Jackson 2016; Manela 2016).

Even when bad things happen, developing gratitude (or appreciation) is often seen as morally good and beneficial. Fitzgerald, coming from a Buddhist orientation, cites the

Dalai Lama as an exemplar of gratitude, noting how he has expressed gratitude to the Chinese government for helping him learn how to love his oppressors amidst the oppression of Tibet (1998). Relatedly, Smilansky (1997) argues one should be grateful whenever people do not harm them, since it is so easy for self-interested people to harm one another in society. These views align with a positive psychology orientation that suggests that maintaining gratitude and appreciation all or most of the time leads one to be more kind, sociable, generous, happy, and caring (Jackson 2021).

In education and society, it is commonplace across cultures to encourage children to regularly feel and express gratitude and reflect on opportunities for gratitude (Carr 2015; Carr, Morgan, and Gulliford 2015). A typical early informal or formal lesson in gratitude is guiding children to say thank you and write letters to benefactors, such as grandparents for toys or guests who visit class. Internalization of a feeling of gratitude is meant to take place here, as the concept and attitude are normally foreign to a toddler but seen to develop over time as a deeply felt emotion (Jackson 2021): "I don't even want these boring socks from grandma."—"Well, you need to be thankful and say 'thank you'; it's the right the thing to do."

The Jubilee Centre develops curricula for gratitude, noting that "80% [of people in Britain] believe there is a lack of gratitude in society [and] would like to see more effort spent on promoting gratitude, particularly in educational and workplace contexts" (Arthur et al. 2015: 5). One handbook requires that students write in journals about grateful experiences, write and send thank-you letters, reflect on experiences of giving thanks to benefactors, and explore how they can benefit from difficult experiences and be grateful for challenges (Kristjánsson et al. 2017). Such practices are supported by psychological research. In one study, one group of students received two weeks of daily interventions in which they were asked to list five things they were grateful for. Another group was asked to list five things "that annoy or bother you" (Froh, Sefick, and Emmons 2008: 220). After three weeks, the researchers found that the first group reported more gratitude, optimism, life satisfaction, and satisfaction with school than the second.

In general, these kinds of interventions focus on individual experiences—that is, on what an individual receives, appreciates, or is grateful for. In lessons created by Character First Education, a US-based organization (2019a), students are asked to describe what a grateful person does and indicate that they will feel and express gratitude: "I will appreciate the people in my life"; "I will write thank you notes." A "Gratefulness Story" describes how Abraham Lincoln had gratitude despite hardships, such as his sister dying (Character First 2019b). An older version of the curriculum (1997) asks students to wear blindfolds and try to make simple drawings to appreciate "the benefit of eyesight" (9). In all these cases, there is less of a focus on relationships or social events or problems and more of a focus on an individual's experiences and expressions.

Yet as with happiness and empathy, having gratitude is not always morally good. As Carr argues (2015: 1483), "just as promotion of or habituation in courage and temperance has produced brave and self-controlled villains and crooks, it could be that sincere, heartfelt and well-judged gratitude might be inculcated or promoted to ends that are quite corrupt or self-serving." A person should not have gratitude if someone murders her sports rival. This may seem obvious, but it is often neglected in lessons that approach gratitude individually and instrumentally, without reflecting on the need for practical judgment.

Relatedly, gratitude as appreciation can take darker forms, of self-satisfaction and joy as a response to others' misery (Jackson 2016, 2017b). In the lesson on eyesight, the student is not asked to reflect on what it means to lose one's eyesight or consider the disadvantages those face who experience vision impairments. Instead, they are only asked to think about themselves as lucky in relation to their unearned capacity. Indeed, many examples given in gratitude chronicling reference privileges, like being given gifts by parents and having a comfortable home. However, one should not simply learn to feel good about having more than others (Jackson 2016, 2017b). Inequality, disadvantage, and disability in society should also be carefully thought about and taught about.

Teaching students that they should feel gratitude when they experience challenges and injuries also has troubling implications. Yes, one can *theorize* about how such gratitude *could* be beneficial. But to teach children and young people that they should in the first place develop gratitude when they face personal problems is another matter (Jackson 2021). If harmful experiences and situations can or should simply (or quickly) be reframed as beneficial, then why should a person work to stop or prevent them? While one may be able in some cases to benefit from gratitude in relation to (learning from) harm, abuse, and oppression, promoting gratitude in such situations can lead people to accept and tolerate injuries and mistreatments, neglecting their own self-respect needs. Promoting gratitude may benefit some people who have faced and overcome challenges, but this is not always—or even normally—the case.

While praising the Dalai Lama's gratitude, Fitzgerald (1998) also elaborates how women can benefit from learning from experiences of abuse at the hands of their fathers. Again, philosophers may find such examples theoretically interesting, but educationally they can be dangerous. (It is also unfortunate and disturbing how frequently violence against girls and women is framed as a context for cultivating virtue, such as in Fitzgerald [1998] and Nussbaum [2016]— in effect seriously risking normalizing such violence through nonchalantly writing about these problems as "interesting" thought experiments where having a good attitude is helpful.)

From a psychological view, people who have suffered from abuse from caregivers often experience expectations for gratitude toward others alongside intense negative feelings of fear and anxiety (Jackson 2021). Furthermore, knowing that gratitude is *expected* and is *supposed* to feel and be good, people with such mixed experiences can face expectations for gratitude as coercive and harmful, leading to confusion, shame, and embarrassment. Such challenges are not easy to address, even by expert therapists. Thinking of education, in the typical classroom there could be one or more students facing such risks and challenges related to gratitude being painful and coercive, such as living with family members who are abusive to them or others. Such possibilities should make educators think twice before expecting all students to frequently and emphatically express gratitude to parents, for example, in case they could accidentally be setting the stage for the toleration and acceptance of harm and increasing harm.

There are also noteworthy differences in experiences of and perspectives on gratitude cross-culturally. In the United Kingdom, people commonly feel more shame, indebtedness, and other negative feelings with gratitude, in contrast with people in the United States and Australia, who more often experience it as basically pleasurable (Morgan, Gulliford, and Carr 2015). Christians express valuing gratitude more than non-Christians in Britain (Arthur et al. 2015: 15). In Chinese thought, gratitude is more often conceptualized as a long-term commitment within an interpersonal relationship with caregivers and authority figures such as educators (Chen and Caicedo 2018). As one saying describes it, "the favor of a drop of water has been rewarded with the gratitude of a fountain of water" (Chi and Hong 2017). In this case, a sense of mutual indebtedness is seen as ideal to deepen connections, bind people together, and build social cohesion, although such an expectation can also be experienced with mixed feelings, as oppressive (Jackson 2021).

Evaluations and expectations related to gratitude also vary by gender. In one study (Arthur et al. 2015), British people were asked to rank how often (1) courage, (2) honesty, (3) kindness, (4) fairness, (5) gratitude, (6) self-control, and (7) humility guided their behavior. Men ranked gratitude last, while women ranked it fourth. As emotions are learned, this suggests that women have been taught to express and feel gratitude to a greater extent than men. On the other hand, for men gratitude has also been found to lead to a sense of burden, given its connection with interdependence (Kashdan et al. 2009). This should also complicate our view of the benefits of encouraging people across situations, cultures, and social positions to have and express gratitude. For instance, in this case boys may benefit less than girls do from simple gratitude lessons (Jackson 2021).

Despite these issues, Jubilee Centre lessons encourage gratitude across contexts and even in the case of challenges (2017). They recommend that teachers use prompts for students, such as "Sometimes you go through a difficult path … ," "Looking back it wasn't all bad … ," "There were some good things to come out of the experience … ," and "In some ways I'm thankful/grateful for what happened because … " (13). Here they note: "Some people in the class may have endured particularly distressing events in their relatively short lives and it is possible this will come to mind. Any children for whom this task becomes upsetting can instead write an entry in their gratitude journal … or create a front cover for their gratitude journal" (Jubilee 2017: 12). It is good to acknowledge that children can face problems in relation to gratitude which should not be treated lightly. However, such children might still feel bad about themselves during such lessons, which continue to suggest that they should try to respond to challenges firstly with gratitude and that they are deviant if they choose not to (or are unable to).

In relation, Gulliford (2018) has provided a better resource for children to explore gratitude and how it can rub against other feelings and issues. *Can I Tell You about Gratitude?* tells the story of Maya, who is thinking about whether and how she should be grateful when her friend gives her a pair of earrings, but then later asks if she can copy (that is, cheat from) her schoolwork. Here, the relationship between gratitude and mixed emotions of indebtedness and reciprocity, and the morality of gratitude more generally can be critically questioned by students, in place of simple lessons that gratitude is always good. Such lessons could be extended by considering how expressions of gratitude and gift giving (and holidays related to thanksgiving) vary across cultures. Students could also explore how even in their classroom they may have learned different things about how and when to say "thank you" at home. Such lessons can help students develop more tolerance for individual and social differences and enable more critical reflection about gratitude in everyday life.

In sum, while gratitude is good in many cases, there are risks in excessively encouraging, expecting, or requiring it in education. The apparent value of always or usually having gratitude can encourage people to ignore or accept problems, harms, and challenges, in their own lives and in those of others. Meanwhile, some groups and individuals are susceptible to having negative experiences of gratitude and should not be encouraged to see gratitude as always a priority. In relation, caution should be taken in expecting children's gratitude for parents, school, and society. Challenges with experiencing and expressing gratitude while developing self-respect are important in life, but they can be overlooked in simple lessons. Thus, a critical exploration of gratitude can help students "appreciate the complex grammar of gratitude discourse" (Morgan, Gulliford, and Carr 2015: 12) and learn to appreciate when gratitude is of use as well as about its potential overuse and abuse.

Conclusion

As a whole, this chapter has observed and questioned the tendency in educating emotions to "accentuate the positive" by dwelling on so-called positive emotions in a simplistic way. As discussed here, happiness, compassion, empathy, caring, and gratitude are worth promoting, encouraging, and exploring in education. However, educating about and for these emotions can also lead to some challenges. Positive emotions and their cultivation are not always the most important thing. They can be challenging to feel and develop sometimes. And the best ways to cultivate them can be different for diverse students. Thus, teachers should take appropriate care in teaching for and about these emotions, and they should not expect or encourage them in every situation. Educators should also allow for and anticipate students experiencing and expressing so-called negative emotions. This will be discussed more in the next chapter.

CHAPTER FOUR

Educating Emotions: Eliminate the Negative?

In the last chapter, we explored so-called positive emotions, noting the risks entailed in educating about and for them in an uncritical, simplistic way. In this chapter, we turn to some of the "negative" emotions that have also been a focus of concern in education. Here, I examine anger, sadness, fear, and anxiety. Paralleling the discussion in the last chapter, I focus particularly on debates about their value in life and education and some of the complications that can arise when teaching about them—in this case, often with an eye to eliminating or diminishing them—in real-life situations. Recognizing diverse experiences is again a focus of our discussion.

Anger

Anger is the most loathed emotion in the world. Western and Eastern traditions discourage anger, describing it in strong terms, as wrong, harmful, irrational, and destructive. The Stoic Seneca observed that anger is usually caused by things beyond one's control (Nussbaum 2016). He concluded that anger is childish, petty, unpleasant, and unhelpful. Religious traditions have regarded anger as a sin: It is "one of the seven deadly sins in Catholicism ... equated with unrequited desire in Hinduism ... one of the five hindrances in Buddhism; in Judaism ... a negative trait; and in the Qur'an ... attributed to Muhammad's enemies" (Peters 2012: 239).

At the same time, anger can also be hard to define. It "may be best defined as a combination of uneasiness, discomfort, tenseness, resentment ... and frustration" (Stearns 1972: 6). It is commonly connected with "envy, jealousy, fury, frustration, annoyance, contempt, and the like" (Averill 2012: 138). Additionally, anger is associated with thoughtlessness and lack of focus and is seen to block experiences of empathy, compassion, and happiness. On the other hand, anger can also be seen to intermingle with some pleasurable, excited feelings, stemming from a self-righteous sense of martyrdom and revenge fantasies (Nussbaum 2016).

Thinking of the sometimes arbitrary experience of anger in our lives can back up the view that anger is dangerously irrational. For instance, "anger can occur for no known reason; it is possible to feel anger and not know why" (Russell and Fehr 1994: 188). People often feel anger that is not related to any real or serious sense of injury or wrongdoing but is more related to minor everyday frustrations (Berkowitz and Harmon-Jones 2004). Changing temperatures in an environment seems to impact (increase) people's sense of anger in experiments, while people commonly experience anger in situations where only they themselves are to blame, as well as in situations where they believe their challenges are reasonable.

A woman may feel angry at herself, and the world at large, for missing a bus. The main (or most direct) reason for her missing the bus was that she hit the snooze button on her alarm many times before getting up, leading to her having insufficient time to get ready for work. In this context, her anger which is irrational and, if anything, caused primarily by her own actions, may lead her to later justify, excuse, or rationalize her strong feelings in terms of external parties victimizing her: For instance, the bus driver arrived and departed from the stop a minute ahead of schedule, while her partner had distracted her with chit chat when she was about to leave. Thus, events apparently conspired to cause the woman to have a bad day.

Often these rationalization and externalization processes which aim to make anger sensible "intensify the anger reaction" unnecessarily (Berkowitz and Harmon-Jones 2004: 115). This intensification can lead to self-destructive, other-blaming thoughts and actions and more and more anger down the road. Upon arriving at work late, the woman's anger (mixed with frustration, embarrassment, and guilt) will make her more likely to become irritated and ashamed when her colleagues recognize or express any annoyance about her tardiness. Then her reaction to her colleagues, that is hardly apologetic or compassionate about the situation, will lead her colleagues to avoid her, thus culminating in a slightly less pleasant day for everyone. In hindsight, no anger is justified or useful here.

Nussbaum thus argues that anger stems from a problematic, questionable perception of injury. Here she recalls her own trivial experiences, such as being angry over "large men, usually very out of shape, who grab one's suitcase without asking permission first and try to hoist it into the overhead rack" on an airplane (2016: 139). Given such contexts and the tendency for anger to lead to revenge "pay back" attitudes and behaviors, Nussbaum (2016) sees anger as irrational and stupid. She recommends transformative "non-anger" through a more rational identification of challenges and their solutions. As she further describes, this non-anger is a practice of self-cultivation and reflection that can enable forgiveness and love. Nussbaum thus urges that "anger must be fought inside oneself" (2016: 147). Nussbaum contends that Martin Luther King, Jr., is a great example of someone who advocated for non-anger. She uses his example, as well as those of Nelson Mandela and Gandhi, who she argues were similarly "not-angry," to educate her readers on thwarting anger.

In schools, anger is likewise commonly seen as negative, undesirable, and distracting. Educational psychologists connect anger with "problematic outcomes, such as difficulties at school, alcohol and drug use, as well as health problems" (Pekrun and Buhner 2014). Thus, anger management and conflict resolution are often encouraged within socioemotional learning and character education (White 2012). As previously mentioned, I learned about anger and "cooling down" in lessons that used images of melting ice cubes, although my friends and I, who seldom had problems with anger, liked to joke instead about eating sweaty cheese.

Another factor which disinclines educators (among others) toward anger is the potential of external parties fueling, manipulating, and exploiting people's anger for their own interests. As media scholars observe, scapegoating in society leads people to focus their anger (for instance, about economic pressures) on others, such as minorities, rather than on political leaders or social and economic systems. In this context, propaganda encourages people to support causes such as ethnonationalism and white supremacy, out of anger and a sense of self-righteousness and aggrieved entitlement (Ahmed 2004b; Kimmel 2017). Here it makes sense to encourage people to think twice before indulging in anger.

In education, lessons often suggest that there is never a good reason to feel or express anger. Character First guides teach that when one is experiencing anger, they should acknowledge pain, forgive others, and not seek revenge or dwell on the past. In one lesson about anger, Corrie ten Boom is praised for practicing forgiveness toward the Nazis after surviving a concentration camp (Character First 2019c). Another lesson praises Abigail Adams for cleaning a dirty ship instead of complaining about it (Character First 2019d). Such lessons teach students not to focus on or sustain anger, but quickly transform it into something positive or productive. The American Psychological Association (APA) also suggests that people focus on relaxation, use humor, and change their environment (2019) when facing anger, echoing strategies discussed for increasing happiness.

However, not all thinkers are intolerant of anger. In contrast with Nussbaum (2016), Aristotle held anger as a virtue, when cultivated "at the right times, about the right things, toward the right people, for the right end and in the right way" (Kristjánsson 2007). While for Nussbaum anger is framed as entirely irrational and counterproductive, Lorde (1984) writes that anger "is loaded with information and energy" (127). Anger can inform a person (that is, the person experiencing it) that something is wrong, and it can communicate information to others in a powerful style when expressed effectively. In this way anger can be useful when one is demanding change in a bad situation. Relatedly, Averill (2012: 141) observes:

> In most everyday episodes, the transgressions that provoke anger are relatively minor—breaking a promise, ignoring a responsibility, being inconsiderate and the like. This fact tends to obscure the role that anger plays in maintaining the social order. No matter how trifling our everyday promises, responsibilities, and considerations may seem to be, they are the threads from which the fabric of society is woven. If they are too frequently broken without mend, society unravels. In a very real sense, then, the many small mendings that are the everyday experiences of anger, each minor in its own right, help sustain a way of life. Anger can be a tool for social change as well as maintenance.

While Nussbaum goes to great lengths to contrast non-anger with "stupid" anger (2016), evaluating appropriate levels and types of anger is challenging in reality. Of course, it is dangerous and unproductive to act directly and exclusively from a sense of blind rage. However, a nuanced consideration of one's anger and its potential justification can lead to morally appropriate responses to problems, where anger is one kind of information source among others (Hildebrand and Jackson 2023). In other words, while uncontrolled rage is irrational and dangerous, apt expressions of anger can have power in "opening up new worlds of sense in which to be creative" (Tessman 2005: 123).

At the same time, there can also be risks in minimizing anger. Srinivasan contends that as "getting angry is a means of affectively registering or appreciating the injustice of the world" (2018: 132), forbidding anger *a priori* in all situations can be a form of affective injustice. From Srinivasan's perspective, rejecting all anger within an unjust society can function as a form of silencing and a refusal to listen to those who may have good reasons to be outraged. Gay relatedly notes (2016) how in conversations about race, white people often accuse and blame people of color for being angry, and "wanting too much or complaining or wasting time or focusing on the wrong things or we are petty or shrill or strident or unbalanced or crazy or overly emotional."

Indeed, angry people of color are regularly stereotyped as uncivilized, dangerous, and disruptive, while white people's anger is rarely regarded as so exceptional. Angry white men's aggrieved entitlement is easy to see in the United States, for example embodied by Donald Trump and his supporters, who regularly expressed anger toward people of color, Latinos, Muslims, and LGBT+ people (Kimmel 2017). Meanwhile, people of color and other minorities are rarely given pedestals in mainstream venues to articulate their concerns or question injustice. Instead, uninvited and unwelcomed by the often-uninterested powers that be, minorities appear to interrupt and "lash out" when they participate in the public sphere. They are thus framed as irrational and threatening when they express concerns, while more privileged people's anger is treated as tolerable or even noble. As Zerilli notes:

> If you search on Google for "shouting down" ... you will find dozens of similar descriptions of uncivil behaviour and the threat to free speech [with] Muslims, gays and lesbians, feminists, racial and ethnic minorities, and other historically disenfranchised groups as the main offenders. .... Whether you interpret these protests as uncivil threats to fundamental political freedoms will depend on whether you think everyone is in fact situated equally in the marketplace of

ideas. ... If some citizens are prone to shout, that may well be because those in power are not listening.

(2014: 111–12)

Girls, women, and people of color are pressured to never be angry or express anger, while boys', men's, and white people's anger is treated as more acceptable. Yet people can also suffer from *losing* their anger. Similar to excessive happiness, a lack of anger can also be unhealthy and pathological (APA 2019). Because some people do not express anger even after being mistreated or harmed, some (like Nussbaum) see anger as a choice. However, psychological damage stemming from experiences of harm and abuse can also impair an accurate sense of hurt and injury. This has been seen among victims of rape and concentration camp survivors (Thompson 2006).

In other cases, people can lose the ability to express anger healthily due to the treatment of their anger as taboo. In this situation, a person may lash out against peers or loved ones who are also victims of wrongdoing, since they cannot safely respond to more blameworthy others (hooks 1995; Lorde 1984). Alternatively, some people may have so much difficulty asserting themselves effectively (or being received fairly) when expressing anger that their experience becomes worse and worse over time, intensifying as a sense of dread, fear, and powerlessness in relation to anger (Ahmed 2004b; Bailey 2018).

In this context, there are significant hidden dangers for philosophers like Nussbaum (2016) and Fitzgerald (1998) and educators in classrooms to promote the idea that one should never be angry. Perhaps there are some individuals out there who have neither the worldly problems nor the normal dispositions which for others lead to everyday trivial and more profound senses of anger. But most of us have reasons, and sometimes good reasons, to be angry. And when some anger can be morally justified, it can reflect a lack of respect for others and harm their sense of agency to forbid or discard their anger as unnecessary and unproductive.

It is true that children are often naturally emotional, and it is part of the work of educators, undoubtedly, to help children learn to understand and better control their emotional reactions. However, forbidding all anger among children will not result in young people who are never angry. Instead, it will merely encourage young people to hide and suppress their anger: to not explore or consider its causes (and, often, the lack thereof), but instead to "hold it in" in shame.

In schools, Kristjánsson (among others) thus advocates for learning about better and worse attitudes toward anger (2007). As he writes, there is "no substitute for anger education ... for each student will acquire a certain disposition to anger, in any case, and we had better ensure that it is the proper one if we are concerned for the student's well-being" (2007: 78). In relation, he recommends considering cases in which anger may be more or less helpful (2007). Instead of only showing how anger is counterproductive and can be suppressed, one can also explore with children how they can express anger productively.

Similarly, Peters argues that young people should learn about how social movements in history have used anger for positive change (2012). Against Nussbaum's suggestion that King and Mandela were not angry and always exercised non-anger, students can explore nuanced descriptions of anger in King's and Mandela's writings (Jackson 2021). They can also watch and listen to civil rights speeches and explore how they might be moved in some cases by speakers' anger—as well as how each of us has different responses, as individuals, to both our *own* anger and the angry expressions of others (Jackson 2021). Here it is not particularly worthwhile to paint an unrealistic picture of non-angry moral saints as role models for the rest of us. In relation, against the stereotypical notion that good Buddhists never have or express anger, students can read Nhat Hanh's work on anger and reflect upon what he means in describing anger as like compost in a garden: not as something to throw away, but as something to use (2001; Yancy and hooks 2015).

Anger is part of life for most of us. It is inevitable in a world where wrongdoings (and annoying and rude inconveniences) are not uncommon. In this case, students should learn that some experiences of anger are normal and potentially useful, healthy, and tolerable—in oneself and in others. In contrast to "take a chill pill" rhetoric, a more complex, mixed perspective on anger is not beyond the grasp of young, growing people. Indeed, it would be an asset in any class focused on issues of justice in a world where many (perhaps all) of us sometimes have good reasons to be angry.

Sadness

Sadness is regarded as the most prevalent negative emotion by psychologists. It can be understood as an emotional pain, involving or related to crying, chest aching, and a feeling of powerlessness or loss. It is primarily believed to occur as a response to a tragic or disappointing event, such as the death of a loved one or a personal failure (Shirai and Suzuki 2017). Like anger, sadness is an umbrella concept. It can involve a variety of states and dispositions, such as grief, nostalgia, despair, depression, and melancholy. We face sadness as part of negative, unavoidable experiences in the world, of loss, death, and heartache.

From a virtue ethics perspective, there can be more and less moral kinds of sadness. For example, sadness over losing an object (say a mobile phone) is not reasonable or moral, although it may not be uncommon (Kristjánsson 2018). In other cases, sadness and grief may not have a clear target (or reason). It is not unusual for people of all ages to feel a bit sad—or sad for a brief period of time—for no obvious or "good" reason. Many people, for example, feel sad during supposedly joyous occasions marking the passing of time or a new phase of life, such as birthdays, holidays, and graduations. Frequent or ongoing experiences of intense sadness are typically regarded more negatively as depression. In this context, an expert view is required to evaluate appropriate versus disordered sadness, as determinations of what is reasonable, useful, and proportionate depend on an individual's situation as well as their usual disposition and tendencies.

In the social sphere, whether sadness is depressing or energizing, or motivating or demotivating, has been debated (Jackson 2021). Sadness is often associated with passive feelings and emotions, of depression, slowness, lethargy, or paralyzing and exhausting grief. Unlike anger, sadness rarely seems to lead to a desire for urgent action, even if one wants to stop being sad. However, sadness and related feelings can also have positive, productive functions. Sadness can help in recognizing and strengthening social bonds and enable communication of pain as well as empathy and kindness (Jackson 2021). Sadness can also shape one's orientation toward the future. For example, sadness over the loss of a family member can inspire a person to more actively express care and concern for living loved ones. Sadness over more minor matters—such as doing poorly on an exam—can teach a person to work harder in the future to get the outcomes they desire. Sadness thus serves, like anger, as a source of information, communicating to the person feeling it that something is not right.

An emotion related to sadness which has been scrutinized in the political domain is nostalgia. As Gotlib writes, "the idea of a backward-looking longing, whose objects are sometimes vague and unclear and sometimes painfully sharp, is nearly universally shared"; it may unfold as "a sadness of something certainly lost; of less easily definable losses; of longings for a past that might, or might not, have been" (2018: 183). Nostalgia for a simpler past marked by a sense of certainty and abundance is often cultivated by politicians. For example, Trump followed Ronald Reagan in suggesting he would "Make America Great Again." In this discourse, allusions are made to calm, peaceful, prosperous suburbs, without poverty, stress, or crime. Yet in the past, there was widespread segregation, racism, sexism, and other forms of deep inequality and injustice. So such nostalgia can be used to promote conservative politics at the expense of more liberal ideals of equality, diversity, and human rights.

Similarly, calls for public mourning, for instance after the death of a politician or after a terrorist attack, can be used to pressure people to support particular causes or join the military (Butler 2004). While some people complain it is not right to "politicize" or exploit tragedies for partisan interests, it is commonplace to be motivated by feelings of sadness, mourning, and grief to want to improve the world around you. For instance, after school shootings in the United States, mourning and grief have often been channeled to engage the community or public in questioning gun laws and thinking more deeply about children's rights and the climate of schools. Thus, practical wisdom is called upon in apt sadness.

While sadness is not always held as negative, educational psychologists regard it as negative in relation to learning. At the same time, due to the common assumption that education should be full of positive emotions, teachers sometimes take on the role of coaches for happiness and optimism when confronted with student sadness (Roberts 2016). Often educational resources designed for managing specific situations involving sadness and grief, for example traumatic events in the school or community such as the death of a student or teacher, encourage moving back into routines quickly and mobilizing youth to improve things (Jackson 2014b). This may include, for instance, learning how to identify and report threats to safety or wellbeing (such as in the case of student suicides or school shootings). Such practices can engage sadness, but they often serve to shift attention elsewhere, leading to the compartmentalization of, or moving on from, sad feelings. How one sees such practices is related to their disposition as they experience specific instances of sadness and tragedy. Some may find meaning in moving on, while others may feel rushed, lost, and alienated by apparent expectations to get on with things.

In this context, the tendency toward repression or avoidance of sadness can be harmful to some young people. In a normal classroom, some students will be sadder for longer and more intensely after a tragedy. And some may feel sad for what seems like no good reason sometimes. However, if a student's sadness is treated by educators as a cause for dismissal or rejection, this is not likely to motivate the student to "snap out of it." Instead, it may lead to their isolation and alienation, which can lead to a worse personal and social situation for them overall. Thus, a student is likely to feel deviant and embarrassed in relation to their sadness, if their teacher does not recognize it as normal and acceptable. And they may become more hesitant to communicate and interact with their teacher and peers about their mixed emotions in the future.

For boys, there also is a risk in dismissing their sadness as feminine or unmanly (Jackson 2021). In schools, "boys learn to suppress sadness" to avoid teasing (Perry-Parrish and Zeman 2011: 146). Boys are more likely to express sadness to girls and to accept girls being sad rather than other boys (Perry-Parrish and Zeman 2011). Parents likewise perceive boys' sadness as more negative and dysfunctional than that of girls. Thus, boys' sadness is often repressed or transformed into anger, which is held as more manly and acceptable. Yet their sadness, which may stem in part from feelings of relationality and caring for others, should also be tolerated, recognized, and seen as normal, rather than mocked or shamed.

Fortunately, sadness is not stigmatized as intensely as anger is. Generally, lessons on sadness balance messages about its normalcy with the hopes (and inevitability) of moving on. For example (Nemours Foundation 2016):

> Everyone feels sad now and then. If you're sad, talking about your feelings can help. When you tell someone how you feel and why, it helps you know that you're not alone in your sadness. It also lets other people know what you need. Saying how you feel helps you get ready to do something that puts you in a happier mood …
>
> When you're in a sad mood, it may seem as if it will last forever. But feelings of sadness usually don't last very

long—often just a few minutes, or maybe a few hours. If you're in a sad mood, there are lots of things you can do to feel better. Exercising and moving around can help relieve a sad mood because being active gets your brain to release chemicals called endorphins that make you feel happier. Listening to upbeat music is another way to help yourself .... Reading a good book, drawing, or playing can help put your mind on something other than what's making you feel sad.

This kind of lesson is not wrong per se, but it does somewhat frame sadness as a distraction in life and education, rather than as something that can be more deeply reflected upon and learned from—as a rich form of life experience in itself. Especially in later years, such a lesson could be complemented by more thoughtful explorations of grief, for example, or of different cultural and religious attitudes to suffering and despair (e.g., Roberts 2016).

Thus, teachers have a valuable role to play as models for accepting, understanding, and caring for people who are sad, not by pushing them aside or asking them to simply cheer up, but by showing through their actions and words that they recognize sadness as normal sometimes for diverse students, who can and will feel sad and express sadness in unique and potentially meaningful ways. This can help all students think more openly about their own sadness and that of others, not as a hurdle to incessant productivity and optimism, but as a provoking part of a rich and vivid life, which can also be enlightening when appropriately reflected upon and responded to.

Fear and Anxiety

In addition to sadness and anger, other challenging emotions that can be stirred up by thoughts and experiences of loss and disappointment are fear and anxiety. Fear is a basic affect, instinctive feeling, and physiological response to a sense of a serious, immediate threat. From a psychological view, it is an essential part of human experience with an important function. Fear is useful when one encounters dangerous animals or anticipates sky diving. Fear provides information that the situation could be harmful. For this reason, common fears are snakes, heights, natural disasters, and dental treatment. Just imagining these things can invoke feelings of dread and panic, at the thought of something terrible happening to oneself, such as death or injury (McNeill et al. 2012). On the other hand, pathological fear is seen as out of proportion to risks and disruptive to functioning (for instance, having a paralyzing fear of being in a classroom, meeting friends, or seeing butterflies).

For most, fear is relatively uncommon—in comparison with anxiety. Anxiety "is a fear reaction to a distal or non-present threat, and so is more cognitive in nature" (McNeill et al. 2012: 161). As mentioned previously, a small amount of anxiety can be a good thing. It can motivate people to do their best, aware of the potential consequences of failure. This can lead to working harder, being more aware and thoughtful, and increasing focus. Yet anxiety can sometimes go too far. Excessive focus can transform into paralysis or lack of control. Too much anxiety can lead to withdrawal, unresponsiveness, freezing up, and submissiveness. Withdrawal and unresponsiveness disable education as an interactive, learning-oriented process. Freezing up and submissiveness are problematic for developing and maintaining a sense of agency and wellbeing (Jackson 2021). For these reasons, educators focused on ameliorating undue student anxiety may give advice on general emotional self-regulation or for specific situations—for example, for test anxiety or public speaking.

From a virtue ethics perspective, to combat excess fear some also advocate for courage. Courage has been explored and promoted by thinkers in Ancient Greece and Rome, in the Middle Ages, in Confucian, Hindi, and Islamic texts, and by existentialists. However, not all people see courage in the same way. In Western philosophy, courage has been defined as the ability or disposition to fear "the right things, in the right way" (Roberts 2017: 23). As mentioned previously, evaluations of situations should be part of taking courage, as courage on the battlefield and courage at a buffet require different things. Here, examining the place and reasonableness of fear in relation to risks and challenges is essential to act with courage intelligently (Sreenivasan 2020). On the other hand, John F. Kennedy's 1956 text *Profiles in Courage* elaborates courage as a kind of resoluteness, to persevere no matter what (Jackson 2021).

An unquestioning, simplistic sense of courage as resoluteness in the face of challenges is often promoted in education (Jackson 2021; Stengel 2018). Character First Education provides several related lessons on courage. In one, past President John Quincy Adams is noted for his "honorable conduct, devotion to justice, and willingness to speak the truth" for presenting fifteen petitions to end slavery. The story concludes that "Adams died in 1848. Seventeen years later and after a terrible civil war, Congress finally ended slavery" (Character First 2019e). This story suggests that Adams is commendable for courage and speaking out against injustice, without considering how in other cases stubbornly staying steadfast in one's beliefs may not be the best path forward (for instance, when one is committed to racist beliefs). Logically, the lesson is not quite on target, while it evades a complex exploration of what courage really consists of in everyday life. It also portrays courage as a manly virtue, reflecting stereotypes that men need to be brave and resolute no matter what (Jackson 2021).

Another Character First story relates the experience of Black men fighting for the north in the United States civil war, despite hearing that "the Confederate Congress has said that any black man caught in army uniform will be executed" (Character First 2019f). Half of these men are "lost" in battle. Yet the text concludes "the men … served their country well and stood firm—for the glory of freedom." Courage is also emphasized in Jubilee Centre curricula on "Knightly Virtues" (Arthur et al. 2014). In these curricula, courage is related to the life of Anne Frank and defined as "having the strength and will to know what you should do even though you may be afraid" (Jubilee Centre n.d.c). Again, these curricula risk teaching the wrong lessons. They prize and idealize "heroic" courage and obscure consideration of more everyday situations, as well as other lessons stemming from these historical events related to morality, ethics, and justice.

In the United States, educators focus on managing fear and anxiety in relation to school shootings. As previously mentioned, systems to prevent and deal with shootings are introduced into schools, which involve (for instance) profiling of potential shooters and students learning what to do when a shooting situation occurs (Borum et al. 2010). Unfortunately, such measures often increase rather than decrease student fear and anxiety. Students are taught what to do in case of a shooting. Yet these interventions expose vulnerabilities to attack and increase thoughts and awareness about risks (Burns and Crawford 1999; Borum et al. 2010; Jonson 2017). These lessons also distract from possibilities to intervene in the situation in more systematic ways, for example, through banning the public sale of assault weapons.

More informally, fear and anxiety are sometimes used by teachers, in some cases unintentionally, as motivational tools. For instance, a teacher might lecture that students are not going to succeed throughout life if they do not do their homework or ace examinations. When I was in school, it was common for teachers, out of frustration, to threaten some students that they would only be able to get jobs at McDonald's, whenever they goofed off in class. Fear of future environmental and climate disaster may also be enabled in schools, to motivate young people to be environmentalists and engage in sustainable behaviors (Dahlbeck 2013).

Similarly, fear and anxiety are encouraged by some politicians and in the media. Search online for foods that can kill you, and you will see right away how news media exaggerate risks about all the things you can eat and die from. Meanwhile populist political discourse and mainstream news media paint pictures every day of more horrific doomsday scenarios, to make losing one's job, criminal foreigners, and war and terrorism seem like ever-present threats (Wodak 2015). While news media may paint terrifying pictures in part to attract an audience (and earn advertisement funding), politicians also justify goals such as cutting welfare, engaging in military interventions, and implementing invasive security apparatuses through cultivating a climate of fear (Jackson 2014b, 2021).

Fear and anxiety can be motivational to help people avoid dangers and risks and be safe. However, too much fear and anxiety can decrease a person's quality of life and their capacity to improve it. In this case, teachers should be careful about fear and anxiety in education and try not to add to it. For example, when it comes to fearsome images from media (including school materials like textbooks), teachers can help students understand how and why media cultivate fear and anxiety as part of literacy education (Jackson 2014b). Furthermore, teachers should avoid exploiting student fear and anxiety, even if well-intentioned, for example, by suggesting that students will not get into university if they do not perform well on the next test. While some want to harness fear for good ends, manipulative tactics and increasing anxiety do not facilitate emotional wellbeing and socioemotional development.

More generally, as with the other emotions reflected upon here, fear, and anxiety should be explored, reflected upon, and taught about in education, rather than either being (often unconsciously) encouraged or dismissed. In classrooms, it is worth discussing with students how fear and anxiety can be used and abused. And like other emotions, their fluidity and dynamism in everyday experience should also be acknowledged in place of expectations that students should (or should not) feel them during various situations. Instead of echoing or ignoring potentially harmful messages that promote fear and anxiety, educators can offer a more reflective response.

Conclusion

We experience so-called negative emotions in nuanced ways in our lives. Sometimes (although not always) we have good reasons for them. However, in education there is a tendency to simplify the complexity of negative emotions to fit them into a limited number of informal and formal lessons, given schooling's diverse aims and an overcrowded curriculum. As with so-called positive emotions, I have challenged us to think more critically about the benefits and risks of negative emotions, of anger, sadness, fear, and anxiety. In relation, I have encouraged us to think more about how we can help young people as they face these emotions in diverse situations in school and society. Finally, I have argued that we should neither teach *against* nor *dismiss* these experiences. We can do more and better to help students understand the value of all emotions, not just the "good ones," in everyday life.

CHAPTER FIVE

Putting It Altogether: Rethinking Educating Emotions

In this book, we have considered different views of emotions across fields and around the world. We have also explored the ways that so-called positive and negative emotions are handled and taught about in education and society, in formal and informal ways. In this chapter, I make some final comments on educating emotions in light of this examination. First, I query discourse on emotional wellbeing in education in relation to three dispositions that have arisen in popularity in recent years: resilience, mindfulness, and grit. Here I scrutinize what these dispositions are and what the purpose of their promotion is in education. I then conclude the text with broader reflections on the politics of the inward turn and the importance of preparing young people to be good actors, not just good *feelers*, in the world around them.

Education for Wellbeing and the Rise of Resilience, Mindfulness, and Grit

Education for emotional wellbeing has become a concern of policymakers in many parts of the world. But in this text I have questioned how to best educate emotions, given the lack of consensus about what emotions are, what is happiness (for instance), and what emotions people should have, and how. I have found that there is no single understanding of education for emotional wellbeing. Rather, people seek out and design education about emotions in response to a variety of challenges and interests. Thus, "emotional wellbeing" seems to stand in for an array of dispositions, attitudes, and expressions sought in young people. Sometimes the purpose of education for wellbeing seems to be more related to the needs of classrooms or schools or general expectations in society, rather than the long-term wellbeing of students.

In relation to education for wellbeing, resilience, mindfulness, and grit are three buzzwords that have exploded in popularity in recent years. Each of these terms has emerged in policy and scholarly discourse as a tool or instrument for education for emotional wellbeing, pointing to specific skills or capacities related to emotions which can be valuable in school and life. However, what these capacities are, and what policymakers aim to do by introducing them in education, deserves scrutiny. Considering each in turn and how they relate to each other can shed additional light on the politics of the inward turn.

In recent decades, *resilience* has become highly sought in education (Cigman 2012; Ecclestone 2012). While not traditionally framed as an emotion or virtue (historically, it has been defined as a quality of environmental or other complex systems), resilience as discussed in education invokes *some* emotional states and precludes *others*. With resilience, strong emotional reactions to challenges, like anxiety and fear, are evaded through staying calm, focused, and rational. In education, resilience is thus valued to deal with negative student emotions and develop more positive ones.

The most well-known resilience curriculum is the Penn Resiliency Program (Jackson 2021). According to program materials, "decades of empirical studies indicate that the program: increases wellbeing and optimism, reduces and prevents depression, anxiety, and conduct problems, results in fewer substance abuse and mental health diagnoses, and improves physical health" (2019). The program focuses on self-awareness and the ability to change one's emotions, making resilience similar to emotional intelligence. It also aims to avoid "catastrophizing" and wasting "energy ruminating," and distract from upsetting situations (Penn Program 2019). Penn offers interventions that teach young people "to change the beliefs that are fuelling their maladaptive emotions ... to keep a sense of perspective; to 'think outside the box' and more flexibly about the multiple and varied causes of problems ('self-disputing') and to restrict the tendency to 'catastrophize' that fuels negative thoughts" (Roberts 2009: 20–1). Another program, the Resilience Framework (Merseyside Youth Association 2019), provides students with a scale of "acceptance," to focus on "what needs to happen and getting on with it, rather than complaining about how we wish things were different."

Meanwhile, educators and psychologists define *mindfulness* as nonjudgmental awareness and present-minded inner focus (Dreyfus 2011). Mindfulness is like resilience, in that it helps instill an accepting, less emotional, negative, or dramatic attitude toward challenges. Mindfulness practices such as meditation and yoga aim to sustain focus on one's mind or body, "on mental contents of particular objects, such as the breath, a sound, or a visual percept" (Greenberg and Harris 2011). The goal is to experience consciousness deeply and in an accepting way, recognizing emotions, impulses, and affects, and observing thoughts which arise (Jackson 2019c). This invites self-knowledge and can make one less sensitive to changes. Meditation and yoga can also be used to develop compassion or empathy, patience, an open mind, and a letting go of troubling thoughts (Jackson 2021).

In contrast to the image of the peaceful and stoic Buddhist monk meditating, mindfulness training is used across fields today, and even by the military, to enable people to focus and succeed against the odds (Hyland 2015). In schools, meditation and yoga are recommended to enhance wellbeing

(Schwimmer and McDonough 2018). Studies report that meditation can reduce social-emotional and behavioral problems; decrease anxiety, anger, stress, and neuroticism; and increase memory, optimism, social skills, emotional regulation, and contentment (Greenberg and Harris 2011; Meiklejohn et al. 2012). Similar benefits are observed of yoga (Bazzano et al. 2018; Serwacki and Cook-Cottone 2012). Montessori schools emphasize mindfulness to develop "concentration skills, independence, and intrinsic motivation" (Montessori 2017). Children engage in a meditation called "walk the line," where they focus on "shifting their weight from one foot to the other, balancing, and being supported by the floor beneath them" (Montessori 2017). Other activities include practicing silence and becoming more aware of one's surroundings. The Jubilee Centre also encourages Buddhist loving kindness meditation, as discussed previously.

Like resilience and mindfulness, *grit* is not an emotion, but a disposition which interrelates with emotional states. Duckworth (2016) defines grit as a combination of passion and perseverance in the face of challenges. She additionally describes it as related to self-control and conscientiousness. Duckworth's "Grit Playbook" recommends the development of grit in education, stating that "grittier students are more likely to graduate from high school" (Stokas 2015). Duckworth suggests that teachers can cultivate grit by modeling, celebrating, and enabling it, with an emphasis on facing challenges. SRI Education, an organization funded by the United States Department of Education (2018), recommends that educators for grit "frame failure as an act of learning" and treat challenges as "inevitable for success" (Jackson 2021).

However, research on the benefits of cultivating these dispositions has not been convincing thus far. Independent studies of the Penn program question its positive results and have found "little to no traces in the next academic year" (Challen et al. 2010: 4). McGee and Stovall (2015) found that during lessons on resilience, resilient students produced *more* stress hormones, suggesting they may "compromise their mental and physical well-being by being resilient" (502). Meanwhile, resilience education can lead to negative feelings of insecurity in students identified as "targets" for lessons (Furedi 2004). This is particularly the case when students are targeted (as they often are) because they are labeled as disadvantaged, for example, coming from poor families or living in poor neighborhoods. Likewise, most studies of mindfulness and yoga have not been rigorous (Jackson 2021). And when it comes to grit, Duckworth acknowledges that results from self-reports can be faked (2016), while "her grit scores are significantly higher for wealthy students than for poor students" (Stitzlein 2018: 7).

It is also worth questioning the moral benefits of resilience, mindfulness, and grit. In general, all three are oriented to *functionality* and achieving external goals, rather than ethics or morality. In lessons on resilience, "what disturbs us are not external things, but merely our 'attitudes' toward them" (Kristjánsson 2013: 209). Similarly, people may be encouraged to be self-centered by some approaches to meditation and yoga, which recommend discarding concern with the world in favor of an exclusive focus on self-care:

> In my opinion, rationale egoism is the proper moral code for a yogi. ... I cherish MY right to life, liberty, and the pursuit of MY Happiness. In self pursuit, I hope to achieve MY inner peace, and with it, the realization that all human beings have the right and capacity to achieve THEIR happiness.
>
> (McGee 2014: 12)

When it comes to grit, McGee and Stovall (2015) observe that grit discourse can undermine Black students by treating racial discrimination as a "path" to grit. Yet "grit framings have yet to respond to racial stereotypes, insults, and assaults" which Black students should not have to continually face— which should be *fought against*, rather than *accepted*, in education (McGee and Stovall 2015: 499).

Indeed, what resilience, mindfulness, and grit share is that they all anticipate students suffering and facing frequent or ongoing challenges. As instruments for responding to and overcoming obstacles, they all regard suffering and challenges as essential—acceptable, tolerable, normal, and natural. On the one hand, it is true that challenges and failures are part of life. No one lives a life without setbacks. Yet there are times when suffering is too great and when challenges are not right— when obstacles should not be seen or framed as opportunities to build grit. Arguably, exploring the potential to change harmful conditions by participating in the world around us is better than promoting suffering to build resilience or grit. Resilience, mindfulness, and grit have their uses, but they also have their abuses. Our emotions are not just "inside" us, but related to and reflective of situations and issues in society at large.

Reconsidering the Inward Turn

When it comes to educating emotions, positive psychology approaches are often recommended and used, because it is believed (indeed, their proponents claim) that they "work." However, I have challenged here "how" they work (in what ways) and whether they do. I mentioned in the first chapter that "mental hygiene" was valued over 100 years ago to "correct" the attitudes of students who did not see education helping them build better lives. In that case, educators said they could either improve society to enhance students' opportunities or change students' attitudes (Boler 1999). They chose attitudes: the *inward turn*. It seems that we are seeing the same choice made today: make students feel good (or fake it!), rather than think more deeply about what youth need, to really be well and have good lives.

Here I have questioned the inward turn view and the notion that emotions (such as happiness) are "inside" us, where we choose them from a menu. As I have explored, our emotions are related to our experiences in the world. In this situation, it is unfair to pin responsibility on individuals for emotions which are related to circumstances they have not created. Yet this is what happens when emotional interventions are used to respond to youth's challenges—particularly disadvantaged youth's challenges. In this context, when poverty and family (and school) factors play a larger role in achievement and wellbeing than student attitudes, schools falsely teach that students as individuals can tackle inequality and others challenges simply by avoiding "catastrophizing," turning away from problems. Furthermore, when "getting on with" the status quo is encouraged, youth victims of unfortunate situations can learn to feel guilty for their reactions to their painful life experiences but not to see or intervene in the environment in a critical way.

As Suissa has noted (2015), the students labeled as in need of resilience or mindfulness or grittiness today were in the 1960s described as "maladjusted." King challenged this language and circuitous logic of demanding youth adjustment to society in a 1967 speech to the APA:

> Certainly, we all want to avoid the maladjusted life. In order to have real adjustment within our personalities, we all want the well-adjusted life in order to avoid neurosis, schizophrenic personalities. But … there are certain things in our nation and in the world which I am proud to be maladjusted. … I never intend to become adjusted to segregation and discrimination. I never intend to become adjusted to religious bigotry. I never intend to adjust myself to economic conditions that will take necessities from the many to give luxuries to the few.

Thus, socioemotional learning approaches which encourage the inward turn risk ignoring what is happening in the world to make students manageable: calm, obedient, and tolerant and accepting of education and society.

Kristjánsson (2013) and Duckworth (2016) have both discussed the inward turn as the "chicken-or-egg" question.

Should educators concerned with wellbeing encourage students to work on *themselves* or on *society*? Kristjánsson has reasoned:

> The question of what should logically come first, the cultivation of positive personal traits or the creation of positive institutions, is a chicken-or-egg question. The important thing is not to waste time wondering where to start but rather to start somewhere. And because it is usually easier to administer personal change … than large-scale political transformation, there are good pragmatic reasons for starting at the individual level.
>
> (2013: 65)

It may seem pragmatic to intervene on individuals, since we are rarely taught to think critically about social systems and how we can make a difference in relation to them. However, this view assumes that interventions and lessons focused on individuals "work" in positive ways. I have contested this here.

Choosing the inward turn also overlooks the way that this discourse is actively exploited by bad actors to frame choices that serve their own interests as good for other people. In 2019, the Ontario Education Minister Lisa Thompson defended cuts to teachers and increased class sizes (from twenty-two to twenty-eight students per class) across schools on the basis that doing so would bolster resilience, "preparing them for the reality of post-secondary as well as the world of work" (Draaisma 2019). As it was put: *larger class sizes would make students more resilient.* In this instance, resilience was promoted to *worsen education*, as students subjected to *worse education* would require *more resilience.* This is inward turn discourse corrupted in the extreme. As discussed previously, more resilient students may not have enhanced wellbeing. Such issues should encourage our skepticism in relation to the inward turn as a political tool, not just a pragmatic way of fixing children's "internal," "personal" problems.

Thus, by zealously supporting the inward turn, governments and schools encourage (informal and formal) lessons that put responsibility on youth to develop and demonstrate "positive" emotions and emotional wellbeing regardless of environments or situations, as if students grinning and bearing it all is the only way to enhance their lot in life. Meanwhile, these discourses ignore backwash effects and counterevidence that challenges whether and how such programs actually "work" (Jackson 2021). And they push aside the idea that politics or society are related to wellbeing, favoring the view that it is all up to individuals. Youth wellbeing is indeed vital. However, its significance is not well reflected in the narrow way it is often thought about and taught about, as an individual responsibility.

Final Thoughts

This book has explored emotions in education and society from various perspectives. To develop in-depth understanding, I have used examples considering many emotions, including happiness, sadness, fear, gratitude, empathy, and compassion, as well as some educationally relevant emotion-related dispositions, such as resilience, grit, and mindfulness. Overall, I have given a complicated account about the nature of emotions and educating for and about them. I have argued that educating emotions is not straightforward, given diversity and complexity in experiences, expectations, identities, and norms related to emotions in society.

How to manage and cultivate emotions has been examined by thinkers around the world, because emotions are important to our lives. Over time, many models have been developed to make sense of emotions and how one can enhance their own emotions and those of others. These models have shaped practices to help people manage their emotions and cultivate more positive and pleasant emotional experiences in schools and other domains (Jackson 2021). With transformations in knowledge and culture, models have shifted and changed.

While some have prevailed over others, no single model has gained universal acceptance and consensus.

In history, some have been attracted to views that highlight emotions' mystery or the divine. Others connect emotions to freedom or enlightenment. Meanwhile, others have felt certain that being a good person requires managing and controlling emotions and rationally directing them. Given the diversity of views, it is not likely that one model will prevail in the future. This is because these are not matters where empirical data can light the way. These matters are subjective. They relate to understandings of goodness, morality, God, and flourishing (Jackson 2021).

But this does not mean that people can or should do nothing when it comes to their emotions. Models for understanding emotions and techniques to enhance emotions have emerged over time in part because they have worked and continue to work, to some extent, for some people. More broadly, part of learning to be a human involves entering into the cultural and social norms of a family and a community. Emotional experiences, expressions, and relations are deeply embedded in these practices.

Thus, emotions are involved in education, whether we like it or not. Emotional education, whether conducted formally or informally, aims to enhance personal and social life, leading to flourishing individuals and communities. It aims to develop "affective equality," recognizing it as a moral and political problem that not all people have equal opportunities to be emotionally well and experience a range of emotions. Hardly anyone wants to feel bad. Yet across societies young people (and older people) grapple with anxiety, depression, fear, anger, distress, and other personally and socially challenging experiences. The obvious solution is to help people learn how to cultivate more positive emotions. It seems that we can help each other, and we must.

Yet given the diversity of views and experiences, a "one size fits all" approach does not work. What works for one person may not work for another. Worse, what works for one may be negatively experienced by another. An educator aiming to promote happiness in their classroom may help some students, while others experience mixed feelings. There is also a risk that some emotional education can worsen affective inequality. As expectations about emotional experiences and expressions vary in societies by gender, race, class, and more, diverse students face nuanced challenges in cultivating a range of emotions. This means educators must grapple with complex issues in educating emotions formally and informally.

The evidence is not persuasive that today's model approaches to increasing happiness, compassion, and gratitude through educational interventions help all (or many) students to feel better in the long run—or become more moral. It is likely in many cases that students learn that gratitude or happiness or resilience is "good" in the views of their educators (among others). However, the internal development processes (or lack thereof) underneath the surface remain unclear. Worse, some interventions have negative effects. Some students experience stigmatization, aware that they do not feel the way they should according to their teachers and peers, possibly enabling a sense of alienation, deficiency, and hopelessness (Boler 1999).

In the case of resilience and grit, some resilient and "gritty" students experience more negative stress than less resilient or gritty students, suggesting that these discourses primarily serve to encourage students to suppress or repress negative experiences, but not to battle effectively against real-life challenges. It should be unsurprising that when our challenges are related to events outside ourselves in the world around us, we are not going to resolve them simply by feeling better "inside." In this case, cultivation of resilience and related dispositions can lead to *more* rather than *less* negative experiences down the line.

Meanwhile, prevalent discourse discourages negative reactions which can often be useful and reasonable in relation to challenges faced in the world. Instead, there is an appeal to turn away from the negative. Such practices may work to make students more manageable. However, they do not reflect the importance of students' needs to develop autonomy and agency and respond critically to problems by reacting in the world beyond the classroom. Thus, many so-called best practices for education for emotional wellbeing ignore the value and power of making a difference, by encouraging young people to only look within.

In reality, there is no "chicken-or-egg" problem when it comes to educating emotions. Education must prepare young people to live in the existing world while also becoming the authors, creators, and leaders of the future. Studying and cultivating good action, not just good feelings, is therefore vital if schools are to develop young people as good actors. Here, teachers should develop a balance between emotional and social education, to support young people with good character and good behavior. And good behavior does not just mean sitting still and being obedient and smiling. It also means facing, responding to, and questioning harm and injustice, and taking reflective action in relation to challenges.

In schools, students can be encouraged to understand what emotions are in their complexity: that emotions are fluid and dynamic; that they can sometimes be difficult to define or distinguish; that they can be loosely or directly related to understandings, beliefs, and perceptions; and that sometimes it can help to "work" on them, while at other times there are more benefits in accepting them. There is no need to teach otherwise. Additionally, students can learn that they can help others around them by appreciating that emotions are experienced in diverse and complex ways in and across communities; that others will not feel the same way that they feel; and that it is valuable in this case to work to actively recognize and understand differences in emotional experiences, expectations, and expressions. This might sound like a lot in kindergarten, but in this text I have mentioned many simple ways these lessons can be imparted in place of less helpful ones.

I hope that readers of this text have found new tools to discuss emotions in these pages. Readers can use ideas from this text to challenge status quo understandings that our emotions are there mainly to help us "get on" with life and succeed in personal or societal goals. The more complicated story of emotions here can lead to expanded conversations at work and at home about what matters in life. More broadly, I hope this text inspires readers to dwell philosophically on what it really means to be a person in the world, where for many of us anxieties, fears, grief, frustration, and an array of other mysterious, wonderful, and challenging emotions strike us, whether we would like them to or not.

Emotions are a big part of our lives—of what it means to be human. Our emotions help characterize our judgments about our experiences, day by day and year by year. They shape how we connect with and treat others. Meanwhile, the pleasantness or painfulness of our emotional experiences is sometimes at the mercy of the outside world, at the mercy of our friends and loved ones (and unfortunately sometimes our bosses). Yet given the importance of emotions in our lives, how often do we talk about them? Is the language we have to talk about our emotions inclusive and thoughtful, or does it make all of us feel sometimes like we are doing something wrong? I hope this book is a breath of fresh air for those who sometimes feel like they are doing it wrong. I hope we all continue learning about emotions in a fruitful way every day. This book is one step to start.

REFERENCES

Ahmed, S. (2004a), *The Cultural Politics of Emotion*, Edinburgh, Edinburgh University Press.

Ahmed, S. (2004b), "Affective Economies," *Social Text*, 79 (2): 117–39.

Ahmed, S. (2010), *The Promise of Happiness*, Durham, Duke University Press.

Alloy, L. B. and L. Y. Abramson. (1988), "Depressive Realism: Four Theoretical Perspectives," in L. B. Alloy (ed), *Cognitive Processes in Depression*, 223–65, New York, The Guilford Press.

American Psychological Association (APA). (2019), *Anger*, APA Online.

Aristotle. (1984), *The Complete Works of Aristotle: The Revised Oxford Translation*, ed, J. Barnes, Princeton, Princeton University Press.

Arthur, J., K. Kristjánsson, L. Gulliford, and B. Morgan. (2015), *An Attitude for Gratitude: How Gratitude Is Understood, Experienced and Valued by the British Public*, Birmingham, Jubilee Centre for Character and Virtues.

Arthur, J., T. Harrison, D. Carr, K. Kristjánsson, and I. Davison. (2014), *Knightly Virtues: Enhancing Virtue Literacy through Stories*, Birmingham, Jubilee Centre.

Averill, J. R. (2012), "Anger," in V. S. Ramachandran (ed), *Encyclopedia of Human Behavior*, 37–144, London, Elsevier.

Ayers, A. J. (1936), *Language, Truth, and Logic*, London, Penguin.

Bailey, A. (2018), "On Anger, Silence, and Epistemic Injustice," *Royal Institute of Philosophy Supplement*, 84: 93–115.

Bazzano, A. N., C. E. Anderson, C. Hylton, and J. Gustat. (2018), "Effect of Mindfulness and Yoga on Quality of Life for Elementary School Students and Teachers: Results of a Randomized Controlled School-Based Study," *Psychological Research and Behavior Management*, 11: 81–9.

Bentall, R. P. (1992), "A Proposal to Classify Happiness as a Psychiatric Disorder," *Journal of Medical Ethics*, 18: 94–8.

Berges, S. (2015), *A Feminist Perspective on Virtue Ethics*, New York, Palgrave Macmillan.

Berkowitz, L. and E. Harmon-Jones. (2004), "Toward an Understanding of the Determinants of Anger," *Emotion*, 4 (2): 107–30.

Blum, L. A. (1980), *Friendship, Altruism, and Morality*, London, Routledge.

Boler, M. (1999), *Feeling Power: Emotions and Education*, New York, Routledge.

Boniwell, I. (n.d.), *How to Teach Happiness at School: Sample Well-Being Lessons*, Berkeley, Greater Good Science Center.

Borum, R., D. G. Cornell, W. Modzeleski, and S. R. Jimerson. (2010), "What Can Be Done about School Shootings? A Review of the Evidence," *Educational Researcher*, 39 (1): 27–37.

Brackett, M. A. and S. E. Rivers. (2014), "Transforming Students' Lives with Social and Emotional Learning," in R. Pekrun and L. Linnenbrink-Garcia (eds), *International Handbook of Emotions in Education*, 1368–88, London, Routledge.

Burns, R. G. and C. Crawford. (1999), "School Shootings, the Media, and Public Fear: Ingredients for a Moral Panic," *Crime Law and Social Change*, 32 (2): 147–68.

Butler, J. (2004), *Precarious Life: The Powers of Mourning and Violence*, New York, Verso.

Bywater, T. and J. Sharples. (2012), "Effective Evidence-Based Interventions for Emotional Well-Being: Lessons for Policy and Practice," *Research Papers in Education*, 27 (4): 409–22.

Camus, A. (1988), *The Stranger*, New York, Cambridge University Press.

Carr, D. (2015), "Is Gratitude a Moral Virtue?" *Philosophical Studies*, 172: 1475–84.

Carr, D., B. Morgan, and L. Gulliford. (2015), "Learning and Teaching Virtuous Gratitude," *Oxford Review of Education*, 41: 766–81.

Challen, A., P. Noden, A. West, and S. Machin. (2010), *UK Resilience Programme Evaluation: Final Report*, London, Department of Education.

Character First. (1997), *Gratefulness*, Oklahoma City, Character First.

Character First. (2019a), *Family Connection*, Oklahoma City, Character First.

Character First. (2019b), *Gratefulness Story*, Oklahoma City, Character First.

Character First. (2019c), *Forgiveness*, Oklahoma City, Character First.

Character First. (2019d), *Self-Control Story*, Oklahoma City, Character First.

Character First. (2019e), *Courage Story*, Oklahoma City, Character First.

Character First. (2019f), *Glory of Freedom*, Oklahoma City, Character First.

Chen, J. and C. Caicedo. (2018), *Understanding Quality Guanxi in China—A Study on Vigor Group*, University of Gavle, Master Thesis, Gavle.

Chi, Z. and S. J. Hong. (2017), "*Guanxi* Culture: How It Affects the Business Model of Chinese Firms," in E. Paulet and C. Rowley (eds), *The China Business Model: Originality and Limits*, 19–40, Cambridge, Elsevier.

Cialdini, R. B., S. L. Brown, B. P. Lewis, C. Luce, and S. L. Neuberg. (1997), "Reinterpreting the Empathy-Altruism Relationship: When One into One Equals Oneness," *Journal of Personality and Social Psychology*, 73: 481–94.

Cigman, R. (2012), "We Need to Talk about Well-being," *Research Papers in Education*, 27 (4): 449–62.

Cook, N. (2012), "'I'm Here to Help': Development Workers, the Politics of Benevolence and Critical Literacy," in V. de I. Andreotti and L. M. T. M. de Souza (eds), *Postcolonial Perspectives on Global Citizenship Education*, 124–39, New York, Routledge.

Crittenden, P. (1999), "Justice, Care, and Other Virtues: A Critique of Kohlberg's theory of Moral Development," in D. Carr and J. Steutel (eds), *Virtue Ethics and Moral Education*, 169–83, London, Routledge.

Curzer, H. J. (2017), "Against Idealization in Virtue Ethics," in D. Carr, J. Arthur and K. Kristjánsson (eds), *Varieties of Virtue Ethics*, 53–72, London, Palgrave Macmillan.

Dahlbeck, J. (2013), "Hope and Fear in Education for Sustainable Development," *Critical Studies in Education*, 2: 154–69.

Derntl, B., A. Finkelmeyer, S. Eickhoff, T. Kellermann, D. I. Falkenberg, F. Schneider, and U. Habel. (2010), "Multidimensional Assessment of Empathetic Abilities: Neural Correlates and Gender Differences," *Psychoneuroendocrinology*, 35 (1): 67–82.

Draaisma, M. (2019), "Larger High School Class Sizes Will Make Ontario Students More Resilient, Education Minister Says," *CBC News*, March: 20.

Dreyfus, G. (2011), "Is Mindfulness Present-Centred and Non-Judgmental? A Discussion of the Cognitive Dimensions of Mindfulness," *Contemporary Buddhism*, 12 (1): 41–54.

Dubs, H. H. (1951), "The Development of Altruism in Confucianism," *Philosophy East and West*, 1 (1): 48–55.

Duckworth, A. (2016), *Grit: The Power of Passion and Perseverance*, New York, Scribner.

Ecclestone, K. (2012), "From Emotional and Psychological Well-Being to Character Education: Challenging Policy Discourses of Behavioural Science and 'Vulnerability'," *Research Papers in Education*, 27 (4): 463–80.

Ehenreich, B. (2009), *Bright-Sided: How Positive Thinking Is Undermining America*, New York, Holt & Company.

Ellis, S. J., D. W. Riggs, and E. Peel. (2019), *Lesbian, Gay, Bisexual, Trans, Intersex, and Queer Psychology: An Introduction*, 2nd ed. Cambridge, Cambridge University Press.

Epley, K. (2015), "Care Ethics and Confucianism: Caring through *Li*," *Hypatia: A Journal of Feminist Philosophy*, 30 (4): 881–96.

Fitzgerald, P. (1998), "Gratitude and Justice," *Ethics*, 109: 119–53.

Foot, P. (1967), "The Problem of Abortion and the Doctrine of the Double Effect," *Oxford Review*, 5: 5–15.

Foucault, M. (1979), *Discipline and Punish*, New York, Vintage.

Foucault, M. (1984), *The Foucault Reader*, New York, Random House.

Frey, B. S. (2008), *Happiness: A Revolution in Economics*, Cambridge, MA, MIT Press.

Froh, J., W. Sefick, and R. Emmons. (2008), "Counting Blessings in Early Adolescents: An Experimental Study of Gratitude and Subjective Well-Being," *Journal of School Psychology*, 46: 213–33.

Furedi, F. (2004), *Therapy Culture: Cultivating Vulnerability in an Uncertain Age*, London, Routledge.

Gay, R. (2016), "Who Gets to Be Angry?" *The New York Times*, June: 10.

Gilligan, C. (1982), *In a Different Voice*, Cambridge, MA, Harvard University Press.

Gotlib, A., ed. (2018), *The Moral Psychology of Sadness*, London, Rowman and Littlefield.

Graham, S. and A. Z. Taylor. (2014), "An Attributional Approach to Emotional life in the Classroom," in R. Pekrun and L. Linnenbrink-Garcia (eds), *International Handbook of Emotions in Education*, 96–119, London, Routledge.

Greenberg, M. T. and A. R. Harris. (2011), "Nurturing Mindfulness in Children and Youth: Current State of Research," *Child Development Perspectives*, 6 (2): 161–6.

Greene, J. (2007), "The Secret Joke of Kant's Soul," in W. Sinnott-Armstrong (ed), *Moral Psychology, Volume 3: The Neuroscience of Morality*, 35–80, Cambridge, MA, MIT.

Greene, J. (2013), *Moral Tribes: Emotion, Reason, and the Gap between Us and Them*, New York, Penguin.

Greene, J., L. Nystrom, A. Engell, J. Darlez, and J. Cohen. (2004), "The Neural Bases of Cognitive Conflict and Control in Moral Judgment," *Neuron*, 44: 389–400.

Gulliford, L. (2018), *Can I Tell You about Gratitude?* London, Jessica Kingsley Publishers.

Hand, M. (2018), *A Theory of Moral Education*, London, Routledge.

Hanh, T. N. (2001), *Anger: Wisdom for Cooling the Flames*, New York, Penguin.

Harrison, M. G., J. Ying, F. Yan, and L. Jackson. (2023), "Teachers' Conceptions of Gratitude and Its Cultivation in Schools in China," *Journal of Moral Education*, forthcoming.

Harrison, T., J. Arthur, and E. Burn. (2016), *Character Education Evaluation Handbook for Schools*, Birmingham, Jubilee Centre for Character and Virtues.

Herr, R. S. (2003), "Is Confucianism Compatible with Care Ethics? A Critique," *Philosophy East and West*, 53 (4): 471–89.

Hildebrand, C., and L. Jackson. (2023), "Can Anger Be Both Apt and Intelligent? On Affective Injustice and the Cultivation of Virtuous Anger," forthcoming.

Ho, S. M. Y., W. Duan, and S. C. M. Tang. (2014), "The Psychology of Virtue and Happiness in Western and Asian Thought," in N. Snow and F. V. Trivigno (eds), *The Philosophy and Psychology of Character and Happiness*, 215–39, London, Routledge.

Hochschild, A. (1983), *The Managed Heart: Commercialisation of Human Feeling*, Berkeley, University of California Press.

Hollan, D. (2017), "Empathy across Cultures," in H. L. Maibom (ed), *The Routledge Handbook of Philosophy of Empathy*, 341–52, New York, Routledge.

hooks, b. (1995), *Killing Rage: Ending Racism*, New York, Holt.

Houston, B. (1990), "Caring and Exploitation," *Hypatia*, 5 (1): 115–19.

Hyland, T. (2015), "On the Contemporary Applications of Mindfulness: Some Implications for Education," *Journal of Philosophy of Education*, 49 (2): 170–86.

Hytten, K. and J. Warren. (2003), "Engaging Whiteness: How Racial Power Gets Reified in Education," *Qualitative Studies in Education*, 16 (1): 65–89.

Jackson, L. (2007), "The Individualist? The Autonomy of Reason in Kant's Philosophy and Educational Views," *Studies in Philosophy of Education*, 26: 335–44.

Jackson, L. (2013), "They Don't *Not* Want Babies: Globalizing Philosophy of Education and the Social Imaginary of International Development," in C. Mayo (ed), *Philosophy of Education 2013*, 353–61, Urbana, Philosophy of Education Society.

Jackson, L. (2014a), "'Won't Somebody Think of the Children?' Emotions, Child Poverty, and Post-Humanitarian Possibilities for Social Justice Education," *Educational Philosophy and Theory*, 46 (9): 1069–108.

Jackson, L. (2014b), *Muslims and Islam in US Education: Reconsidering Multiculturalism*, New York, Routledge.

Jackson, L. (2016), "Why Should I Be Grateful? The Morality of Gratitude in Contexts Marked by Injustice," *Journal of Moral Education*, 45 (3): 276–90.

Jackson, L. (2017a), "Altruism, Non-Relational Care, and Global Citizenship Education," in M. Moses (ed), *Philosophy of Education 2014*, 409–15, Urbana, Philosophy of Education Society.

Jackson, L. (2017b), "Questioning Gratitude in an Unequal World with Reference to the Work of Toni Morrison," *Concentric: Literary and Cultural Studies*, 43 (1): 227–43.

Jackson, L. (2019a), "The Smiling Philosopher: Emotional Labor, Gender, and Harassment in Conference Spaces," *Educational Philosophy and Theory*, 51 (7): 693–701.

Jackson, L. (2019b), *Questioning Allegiance: Resituating Civic Education*, London, Routledge.

Jackson, L. (2019c), "Must Children Sit Still? The Dark Biopolitics of Mindfulness and Yoga in Education," *Educational Philosophy and Theory*, 52 (2): 120–5.

Jackson, L. (2021), *Beyond Virtue*, Cambridge, Cambridge University Press.

Jackson, L. (2023), "Being and Becoming in the World beyond Virtue: Behind the Curtain," *Studies in Philosophy and Education*, 42, 563–567.

Jonson, C. L. (2017), "Preventing School Shootings: The Effectiveness of Safety Measures," *Victims & Offenders*, 12 (6): 956–73.

Jubilee Centre. (n.d.a), "Managing Feelings," in *The Character Curriculum*, Birmingham, Jubilee Centre for Character and Virtues.

Jubilee Centre. (n.d.b), *Cultivating Compassion: Learning to Feel, Think and Behave Kindly towards Others (Teacher Handbook)*, Birmingham, Jubilee Centre for Character and Virtues.

Jubilee Centre. (n.d.c), *The Knightly Virtues Pack*, Birmingham, Jubilee Centre for Character and Virtues, https://www.jubileecentre.ac.uk/1641/character-education/resources/knightly-virtues.

Jubilee Centre. (2017), *A Framework for Character Education in Schools*, Birmingham, Jubilee Centre for Character and Virtues.

Kang, S. Y. (2006), "Identity-centered Multicultural Care Theory: White, Black, and Korean Caring," *Educational Foundations*, 20 (3–4): 35–49.

Kant, I. (1970), "Answer to the Question: 'What is Enlightenment?'" in H. S. Reiss (ed), *Kant: Political Writings*, trans. H. B. Nisbet, 54–60, Cambridge, Cambridge University Press.

Kant, I. (1996), *The Metaphysics of Morals, in Practical Philosophy*, trans. M. J. Gregor, Cambridge, Cambridge University Press.

Kashdan, T. B., A. Mishra, W. E. Breen, and J. J. Froh. (2009), "Gender Differences in Gratitude: Examining Appraisals, Narratives, the Willingness to Express Emotions, and Changes in Psychological Needs," *Journal of Personality*, 77 (3): 691–730.

Kesebir, P. and E. Diener. (2014), "A Virtuous Cycle: The Relationship between Happiness and Virtue," in N. Snow and F. V. Trivigno (eds), *The Philosophy and Psychology of Character and Happiness*, 287–306, London, Routledge.

Kimmel, M. (2017), *Angry White Men: American Masculinity at the End of an Era*, New York, Nation Books.

Kohlberg, L. (1981), *The Psychology of Moral Development*, New York, Harper & Row.

Kohlberg, L., C. Levine, and A. Hewer (1983), *Moral Stages: A Current Formulation and a Response to Critics*, London, Karger.

Konarzewski, K. (1992), "Empathy and Protest: Two Roots of Heroic Altruism," in P. M. Oliner, S. P. Oliner, L. Baron, L. A. Blum, D. L. Krebs, and M. Z. Smolenska (eds), *Embracing the Other: Philosophical, Psychological, and Historical Perspectives on Altruism*, 22–9, New York, New York University Press.

Kristjánsson, K. (2007), *Aristotle, Emotions, and Education*, London, Routledge.

Kristjánsson, K. (2013), *Virtues and Vices in Positive Psychology: A Philosophical Critique*, Cambridge, Cambridge University Press.

Kristjánsson, K. (2018), *Virtuous Emotions*, Oxford, Oxford University Press.

Kristjánsson, K., L. Gulliford, J. Arthur, and F. Moller. (2017), *Gratitude and Related Character Virtues*, Birmingham, Jubilee Centre for Character and Virtues.

Kupperman, J. J. (1995), "The Emotions of Altruism, East and West," in J. Marks and R. T. Ames (eds), *Emotions in Asian Thought: A Dialogue in Comparative Philosophy*, 123–30, New York, State University of New York.

Leighton, J. (2011), *The Battle for Compassion: Ethics in an Apathetic Universe*, Oxford, Blackwell.

Li, C. (1994), "The Confucian Concept of Jen and Feminist Ethics of Care: A Comparative Study," *Hypatia*, 9 (1): 70–89.

Liu, Y. (2004), *The Unity of Rule and Virtue: A Critique of a Supposed Parallel between Confucian Ethics and Virtue Ethics*, London, Marshall Cavendish.

Lorde, A. (1984), *Sister Outsider*, Trumansburg, Crossing Press.

Mai, X., et al. (2011), "Eyes Are Windows to the Chinese Soul: Evidence from the Detection of Real and Fake Smiles," *PLoS One*, 6 (5), doi: 10.1371/journal.pone.0019903.

Maki, W. J. (2018), "The Cadence of Nature for Educating: Uncovering a Path to Knowing in a Comparative Study of Daoism and Lost Gospels," *Educational Philosophy and Theory*, 51 (2): 1216–26.

Manela, T. (2016), "Gratitude and Appreciation," *American Philosophical Quarterly*, 53 (3): 281–94.

May, J. (2017), "Empathy and Intersubjectivity," in H. L. Maibom (ed), *The Routledge Handbook of Philosophy of Empathy*, 169–79, New York, Routledge.

McGee, E. O. and D. Stovall. (2015), "Reimagining Critical Race Theory in Education: Mental Health, Healing, and the Pathway to Liberatory Praxis," *Educational Theory*, 65 (5): 491–511.

McGee, K. (2014), "Ethics for Yogis," *Mantra*, 4: 12.

McNeill, D. W., A. M. Vargovich, B. J. Ries, and C. L. Turk. (2012), "Anxiety and Fear," in V. S. Ramachandran (ed), *Encyclopedia of Human Behavior*, 161–8, London, Elsevier.

McRae, E. (2012), "A Passionate Buddhist Life," *Journal of Religious Ethics*, 40 (1): 99–121.

McRae, E. (2015), "Anger and the Oppressed: Indo-Tibetan Buddhist Perspectives," in M. Cherry and O. Flanagan (eds), *The Moral Psychology of Anger*, 105–21, London, Rowman and Littlefield.

McRae, E. (2017), "Empathy, Compassion, and 'Exchanging Self and Other' in Indo-Tibetan Buddhism," in H. L. Maibom (ed), *The Routledge Handbook of Philosophy of Empathy*, 123–34, New York, Routledge.

Meiklejohn, J., C. Phillips, L. M. Freedman, M. L. Griffin, G. Biegel, A. Roach, J. Frank, C. Burke, L. Pinger, G. Soloway, R. Isberg, E. Sibinga, A. Grossman, and A. Saltzman. (2012), "Integrating Mindfulness Training into K-12 Education: Fostering the Resilience of Teachers and Students," *Mindfulness*, 3 (4): 291–307.

Merseyside Youth Association. (2019), *Resiliency Framework*, https://resilienceframework.co.uk.

Miller, C. B. (2014), "The Real Challenge to Virtue Ethics from Psychology," in N. Snow and F. V. Trivigno (eds), *The Philosophy and Psychology of Character and Happiness*, 15–34, London, Routledge.

Monroe, K. R. (1996), *The Heart of Altruism: Perception of a Common Humanity*, Princeton, Princeton University Press.

Montessori Academy. (2017), *Montessori and Mindfulness*, https://montessoriacademy.com.au/montessori-and-mindfulness/.

Morgan, B., L. Gulliford, and D. Carr. (2015), "Educating Gratitude: Some Conceptual and Moral Misgivings," *Journal of Moral Education*, 44: 97–111.

Nagel, T. (1970), *The Possibility of Altruism*, Princeton, Princeton University Press.

Nemours Foundation/ KidsHealth. (2016), *Feeling Sad*, Orlando, Nemours Foundation.

Nesterova, Y. and L. Jackson (2016), "Transforming Service
  Learning for Global Citizenship Education: Moving from
  Affective-Moral to Social-Political," *Revista Espanola de
  Educacion Comparada (Spanish Journal of Comparative
  Education)*, 28: 73–90.

Noddings, N. (1984), *Caring: A Feminine Approach to Ethics and
  Moral Education*, Berkeley, University of California Press.

Noddings, N. (2002), *Starting at Home: Caring and Social Policy*,
  Berkeley, University of California Press.

Noddings, N. (2003), *Happiness and Education*, Cambridge,
  Cambridge University Press.

Nussbaum, M. C. (1994), "Patriotism and Cosmopolitanism,"
  Boston Review, Fall.

Nussbaum, M. C. (2001), *Upheavals of Thought: The Intelligence of
  Emotions*, Cambridge, Cambridge University Press.

Nussbaum, M. C. (2012), "Who Is the Happy Warrior? Philosophy,
  Happiness Research, and Public Policy," *International Review of
  Economics*, 59: 335.

Nussbaum, M. C. (2013), *Political Emotions*, Cambridge, MA,
  Harvard University Press.

Nussbaum, M. C. (2016), *Anger and Forgiveness: Resentment,
  Generosity, Justice*, Oxford, Oxford University Press.

Okin, S. M. (1989), "Reason and Feeling in Thinking about Justice,"
  Ethics, 99 (2): 229–49.

Pekrun, R. and M. Buhner. (2014), "Self-Report Measures of
  Academic Emotions," in R. Pekrun and L. Linnenbrink-Garcia
  (eds), *International Handbook of Emotions in Education*,
  561–79, London, Routledge.

Pekrun, R. and L. Linnenbrink-Garcia, eds (2014), *International
  Handbook of Emotions in Education*, London, Routledge.

Penn Resiliency Program. (2019), *Penn Resilience Program and
  Perma Workshops*, Philadelphia, Trustees of the University of
  Pennsylvania.

Perry-Parrish, C. and J. Zeman. (2011), "Relations among Sadness
  Regulation, Peer Acceptance, and Social Functioning in Early
  Adolescence: The Role of Gender," *Social Development*, 20 (1):
  135–53.

Peters, M. A. (2012), "Looking Forward in Anger," *Educational
  Philosophy and Theory*, 44 (3): 238–44.

Rawls, J. (1993), *Political Liberalism*, New York, Columbia University Press.

Rawls, J. (2000), *Justice as Fairness: A Restatement*, Cambridge, MA, Harvard University Press.

Roberts, P. (2016), *Happiness, Hope, and Despair: Rethinking the Role of Education*, New York, Peter Lang.

Roberts, R. C. (2013), *Emotions in the Moral Life*, Cambridge, Cambridge University Press.

Roberts, R. C. (2017), "Varieties of Virtue Ethics," in D. Carr, J. Arthur, and K. Kristjánsson (eds), *Varieties of Virtue Ethics*, 17–34, London, Palgrave MacMillan.

Roberts, Y. (2009), *Grit: The Skills for Success and How They Are Grown*, London, The Young Foundation.

Rousseau, J. J. (1979), *Emile, or on Education*, trans. A. Bloom, New York, Basic.

Russell, B. (1961), *Religion and Science*, New York, Oxford University Press.

Russell, J. A. and B. Fehr. (1994), "Fuzzy Concepts in a Fuzzy Hierarchy: Varieties of Anger," *Journal of Personality and Social Psychology*, 67 (2): 186–205.

Sarkissian, H. (2014), "Is Self-Regulation a Burden or a Virtue? A Comparative Perspective," in N. Snow and F. V. Trivigno (eds), *The Philosophy and Psychology of Character and Happiness*, 181–96, London, Routledge.

Sartre, J. P. (1943), *Being and Nothingness*, trans. Hazel Barnes, New York, Washington Square Press.

School Speciality. (2018), *Premier Esteem Primary Planner*, Greenville, School Speciality.

Schwimmer, M. and K. McDonough. (2018), "Mindfulness and 'Educational New Ageism'," in K. Hytten (ed), *Oxford Research Encyclopedia of Philosophy of Education*, Oxford, Oxford University Press, https://oxfordre.com/education/display/10.1093/acrefore/9780190264093.001.0001/acrefore-9780190264093-e-175.

Seligman, M. E. P. (2002), *Authentic Happiness: Using the New Positive Psychology to Realize Your Potential for Lasting Fulfilment*, New York, Random House.

Serwacki, M. L. and C. Cook-Cottone. (2012), "Yoga in the Schools: A Systematic Review of the Literature," *International Journal of Yoga Therapy*, 22: 101–10.

Shirai, M. and N. Suzuki. (2017), "Is Sadness Only One Emotion? Psychological and Physiological Responses to Sadness Induced by Two Different Situations: 'Loss of Someone' and 'Failure to Achieve a Goal'," *Frontiers in Psychology*, 8: 288.

Shuman, V. and K. R. Scherer. (2014), "Concepts and Structures of Emotions," in R. Pekrun and L. Linnenbrink-Garcia (eds), *International Handbook of Emotions in Education*, 13–35, London, Routledge.

Simons, J. (1990), *Diaries and Journals of Literary Women from Fanny Burney to Virginia Woolf*, London, Palgrave Macmillan.

Singer, P. (2019), *The Life You Can Save: How to Do Your Part to End World Poverty*, New York, Random House.

Smilansky, S. (1997), "Should I Be Grateful to You for Not Harming Me?" *Philosophy and Phenomenological Research*, 57: 585–97.

Smith, A. (1969), *The Theory of the Moral Sentiments*, Indianapolis, Liberty Classics.

Sreenivasan, G. (2020), *Emotion and Virtue*, Princeton, Princeton University Press.

SRI International. (2018), *Promoting Grit, Tenacity, and Perseverance: Critical Factors for Success in the 21st Century*, Menlo Park, SRI International.

Srinivasan, A. (2018), "The Aptness of Anger," *The Journal of Political Philosophy*, 26 (2): 123–44.

Stearns, F. R. (1972), *Anger: Psychology, Physiology, Pathology*, Springfield Illinois, Thomas.

Stengel, B. (2018), "Practicing Courage in a Communal Key," *Educational Theory*, 68 (2): 213–33.

Stitzlein, S. M. (2018), "Teaching for Hope in the Era of Grit," *Teachers College Record*, 120: 1–28.

Stokas, A. G. (2015), "A Genealogy of Grit: Education in the New Gilded Age," *Educational Theory*, 65 (5): 513–28.

Suissa, J. (2015), "Character Education and the Disappearance of the Political," *Ethics and Education*, 10 (1): 105–17.

Tessman, L. (2005), *Burdened Virtues: Virtue Ethics for Liberatory Struggles*, Oxford, Oxford University Press.

Thompson, S. (2006), "Anger and the Struggle for Justice," in S. Clarke, P. Hoggett, and S. Thompson (eds), *Emotion, Politics and Society*, 123–44, New York, Palgrave Macmillan.

Veenhoven, R. (2008), "Sociological Theories of Subjective Well-Being," in M. Eid and R. Larsen (eds), *The Science of Subjective*

Well-Being: A Tribute to Ed Diener, 44–61, New York, Guilford Publications.

Watson, J. L. (2006), "McDonald's in Hong Kong: Consumerism, Dietary Change, and the Rise of a Children's Culture," in J. L. Watson (ed), *Golden Arches East: McDonald's in East Asia*, 77–103, Stanford, Stanford University Press.

Weber, M. (1959), *The Protestant Work Ethic and the Spirit of Capitalism*, Oxford, Oxford University Press.

Wei, X. (2007), "Caring: Confucianism, Feminism, and Christian Ethics," *Contemporary Chinese Thought*, 39 (2): 32–48.

White, P. (2012), "Making Political Anger Possible: A Task for Civic Education," *Journal of Philosophy of Education*, 46 (1): 1–13.

Wingfield, A. H. (2007), "The Modern Mammy and the Angry Black Man: African American Professionals' Experiences with Gendered Racism in the Workplace," *Race, Gender & Class*, 14 (1–2): 196–212.

Wodak, R. (2015), *The Politics of Fear: What Right-Wing Populist Discourses Mean*, London, Sage.

Wong, B. and L. Jackson. (2023), "Fostering Justice through Education: A Confucian Perspective," in I. Bostad, M. Papastephanou, and T. Strand (eds), *Justice, Education, and the World of Today: Philosophical Investigations*, 155–67, London, Routledge.

Yancy, G. and b. hooks. (2015), "bell hooks: Buddhism, the Beats, and Loving Blackness," *New York Times*, December: 10.

You, Z., A. G. Rud, and Y. Hu. (2018), *The Philosophy of Chinese Moral Education: A History*, New York, Palgrave MacMillan.

Zembylas, M. (2008), "Trauma, Justice, and the Politics of Emotion: The Violence of Sentimentality in Education," *Discourse*, 29 (1): 1–17.

Zerilli, L. M. G. (2014), "Against Civility: A Feminist Perspective," in A. Sarat (ed), *Civility, Legality, and Justice in America*, 107–31, Cambridge, Cambridge University Press.

INDEX